CULTURES OF THE WORLD

Trinidad and Tobago

Sean Sheehan and Yong Jui Lin

mc Marshall Cavendish
Benchmark
New York

PICTURE CREDITS

Cover: © Robert Harding Travel / Photolibrary
alt.type/Reuters: 38, 121 • Audrius Tomonis: 138 • Corbis: 1, 5, 9, 10, 20, 21, 23, 28, 33, 34, 44, 45, 48, 50, 55, 56, 59, 62, 67, 76, 81, 82, 83, 84, 90, 100, 102, 103, 104, 116, 122, 124, 126 • David Simson: 29, 35, 40, 61 • Getty Images: 30, 37, 88, 99, 107, 111, 118, 119, 120, 129 • Haga Library: 27, 31, 60, 66, 87, 95 • Hutchison: 41, 63 • International Photobank: 17 • MCIA Archives: 131 • National Geographic Society: 53 • North Wind Pictures Archives: 22 • Photolibrary: 3, 6, 7, 8, 12, 13, 14, 15, 16, 18, 19, 32, 39, 42, 43, 46, 47, 49, 51, 52, 57, 58, 64, 65, 68, 69, 70, 71, 73, 74, 77, 78, 79, 80, 85, 89, 91, 93, 94, 96, 97, 98, 101, 105, 106, 108, 109, 110, 112, 113, 115, 117, 123, 125, 127, 128, 130 • Trip Photographic Library: 72, 75, 86, 114 • Wikipedia: 11

PRECEDING PAGE

A woman dressed up in her elaborate underwater-theme outfit during a Carnival in Trinidad and Tobago.

Publisher (U.S.): Michelle Bisson
Editors: Deborah Grahame-Smith, Mindy Pang
Copyreader: Tara Tomczyk
Designers: Nancy Sabato, Lock Hong Liang
Cover picture researcher: Tracey Engel
Picture researcher: Joshua Ang

Marshall Cavendish Benchmark
99 White Plains Road
Tarrytown, NY 10591
Website: www.marshallcavendish.us

© Times Media Private Limited 2001
© Marshall Cavendish International (Asia) Private Limited 2011
® "Cultures of the World" is a registered trademark of Times Publishing Limited.

Originated and designed by Times Media Private Limited
An imprint of Marshall Cavendish International (Asia) Private Limited
A member of Times Publishing Limited

Marshall Cavendish is a trademark of Times Publishing Limited.

All Internet sites were correct and accurate at the time of printing. All monetary figures in this publication are in U.S. dollars.

Library of Congress Cataloging-in-Publication Data
Sheehan, Sean, 1951-
  Trinidad and Tobago / Sean Sheehan and Yong Jui Lin. — 2nd ed.
      p. cm. — (Cultures of the world)
  Includes bibliographical references and index.
  Summary: "Provides comprehensive information on the geography, history,
    wildlife, governmental structure, economy, cultural diversity, peoples,
    religion, and culture of Trinidad and Tobago" — Provided by publisher.
  ISBN 978-1-60870-456-9
  1. Trinidad and Tobago — Juvenile literature. I. Yong, Jui Lin.
  II. Sheehan, Sean, 1951- Trinidad & Tobago. III. Title.
  F2119.S54 2011
  972.983—dc22   2010030344

Printed in China
7 6 5 4 3 2 1

CONTENTS

INTRODUCTION

THE ISLANDS OF TRINIDAD AND TOBAGO ARE THE SOUTHERN-most of the Caribbean islands, lying only a few miles off the coast of South America, near Venezuela. They have been attracting settlers for well over two millennia, and this has led to a lively and varied population from many corners of the globe. Europeans, Africans, Indians, and Chinese have all made their homes here, and a racial and cultural melting pot is the result. Unlike in other parts of the world, the blending of cultures has not produced conflict, and the people celebrate their sense of togetherness and national identity. Distinct from other Caribbean islands, Trinidad and Tobago has managed to welcome overseas visitors without selling its soul to tourism and diluting its own cultural identity in the process. The people of Trinidad and Tobago know how to enjoy life and are blessed with a hospitable environment that helps make this possible.

GEOGRAPHY

Sheltering mountains protect the quiet and serene fishing village of Castara in northwestern Tobago.

CHAPTER 1

TRINIDAD AND TOBAGO ARE two relatively small islands off the northern coast of Venezuela in the Caribbean Sea. They are the two southernmost islands of a chain of islands known as the Windward Islands, a chain that includes the islands of Grenada, Dominica, Saint Lucia, and others.

These in turn are part of a 2,000-mile-long (3,218-kilometer-long) chain of islands known as the West Indies, which includes Cuba and Jamaica and stretches from southeast of Florida to the northern coast of Venezuela. The West Indies separate the Caribbean Sea from the Atlantic Ocean.

In addition to the official population, the adjacent region of Port-of-Spain has a population close to 600,000 people.

A lush green valley in Trinidad.

Caroni Swamp is one of the many places in Trinidad where the natural environment is still unspoiled.

Trinidad is separated from Venezuela by the Gulf of Paria, which extends 100 miles (161 km) east to west and 40 miles (64 km) north to south. The island has a total area of 1,864 square miles (4,828 square km) and is the more industrialized of the two islands. Tobago, lying 7 miles (11 km) northeast of Trinidad, is smaller, having only a total area of 116 square miles (300 square km).

TERRAIN

The Pitch Lake is a tourist attraction in Trinidad that attracts 20,000 visitors annually. Extremophiles, organisms that thrive in extreme conditions, live in the Pitch Lake.

The islands of Trinidad and Tobago are basically extensions of mainland South America. Trinidad has three ranges of hills running across it from west to east. The most significant is the Northern Range, part of a range that starts in the Andes Mountains and extends along the Paria Peninsula to the islands. The Northern Range has an average height of about 1,500 feet (457 meters), and its highest point is El Cerro del Aripo (Mount Aripo) at 3,084 feet (940 m). The second range of hills, known as the Central Range, has its highest point, Mount Tamana (1,009 feet/307 m), at the eastern end. The Southern Range follows the southern coast of the island and is largely a series of low hills. Those on the east are known as the Trinity Hills. The low-lying land between the ranges tends to be swampy, fed by the many rivers that run off from the hills. Northwest of the island is the large Caroni Swamp, and in the east of the island the Nariva Swamp.

Three pitch lakes exist in the world. One is in California, another in Venezuela, and the third in Trinidad. Unlike the other two, the Pitch Lake in Trinidad is still active. The Pitch Lake is the largest natural deposit of asphalt in the world, located at La Brea in southwest Trinidad. Pitch lakes occur when oil oozes up to the surface of the ground and the more volatile elements evaporate, leaving a residue of naturally occurring asphalt. Trinidad's Pitch Lake covers 116 acres (47 hectares), is 246 feet (75 m) deep, and is thought to contain 6.7 million tons of asphalt, which is replenished continuously. It is possible to walk across the lake. When Sir Walter Raleigh visited Trinidad in the 16th century, he used the asphalt that he found in the lake to caulk his boats and declared it the best he had ever seen.

In addition to the hundreds of small rivers flowing down its hills, Trinidad has only two major rivers. The Ortoire in the south stretches for 31 miles (50 km) and empties into the Atlantic Ocean. The second major river is the Caroni in the northwest. It rises in the Northern Range and flows 25 miles (40 km) toward the mangrove swamps along the northwestern coast.

Tobago is a further extension of the Northern Range of Trinidad. It has a central ridge that runs southwest to northeast; it is called the Main Ridge.

Sunrays stream through the thick rain forest foliage in Trinidad.

HABITATS

Trinidad and Tobago has an abundant plant and animal life mainly because of the undeveloped nature of the islands and the variety of habitats. Unlike the other islands in the West Indies that are volcanic in origin, these islands form part of the lower slopes of the Andes Mountains. Four ranges of hills, two large rivers and hundreds of small rivers, an extensive coastline, mangrove swamps, and coral reefs provide many habitats for wild creatures.

RAIN FOREST

The four ranges of hills are densely covered with rain forests. The tallest trees form a canopy over the forest that reaches as high as 150 feet (46 m). Orchids and bromeliads grow in the trees, fastened to the branches and taking their nourishment from the air and dying leaves. Lianas wind their way up tree trunks from the ground. The trees of the rain forest tend to flower in the spring, although in the dry season from December to March, an introduced species, the immortelle tree (*Erythrina micropteryx*), covers the forest in orange flowers. In March another tree bursts into bloom—the poui tree, with striking yellow blossoms. Before it flowers, it loses its leaves, making the blossoms all the more striking.

Two-fifths of the land is forested.

Typical savannah vegetation is found in the Aripo Savannah, a nature reserve east of Port-of-Spain. Monica palms grow at the edges of the high grassland, and sundew flourishes in this inhospitable land because it is able to trap insects to provide nourishment. There are many bird species here—hummingbirds, the Savannah hawk, red-bellied macaws, and parrots.

An amazing variety of birds lives in the forest, mainly high up in the canopy where they feed on the fruit of the trees as it comes into season. In the hills, at least 2,000 feet (609 m) above sea level, there are yellow-legged thrush, nightingale thrush, and blue tanagers. At lower levels but less easy to spot is the unusual oilbird (*Steatornis caripensis*), which lives deep in caves and forages for fruit at night. Young oilbirds were once used for both meat and fuel oil, but they are rare now. A large oilbird has a wingspan of 3 feet (1 m). The bird of paradise on Tobago is an introduced species.

The rain forest is also home to a variety of animals. Ocelots that live in the forest often make their way to cultivated land where this protected species is shot by farmers to protect their domestic animals.

The nocturnal oilbirds feed on the fruits of the oil palm and other tropical laurels.

SWAMPLAND

Both Trinidad and Tobago have areas of swampland where rivers meander toward the sea, creating large wet areas that are home to many species of plants and animals. The most characteristic plant life in these areas is the mangrove tree. The tree is able to survive in salt marshes because its roots grow from the trunk above the water line and take in air from the atmosphere. The tree produces seeds that germinate while still attached to the trunk, sending roots into the mud before the seedling falls away from the tree. This prevents the seed from being washed out to sea when the high tide sweeps into the swamp.

The Caroni Swamp in northwestern Trinidad is a nature reserve consisting of 12,000 acres (4,860 ha) of lagoon, forest, and marshland. The scarlet ibis, the national bird of Trinidad and Tobago, lives here in flocks. Among the other 140 bird species to be found at Caroni are the cormorant, anhinga, and boat-billed heron. In the waters of the swamp are edible fish and other marine life, including huge garrupas, snappers, tree oysters, mussels, and blue crabs. The caiman, a type of crocodile, also lives in the swamp. Iguanas and manatees can also be found.

The scarlet ibis is the national bird of Trinidad and is featured on the Trinidad and Tobago coat of arms. These elegant creatures nest in the tropical swamps and feed on fish, frogs, reptiles, and crustaceans.

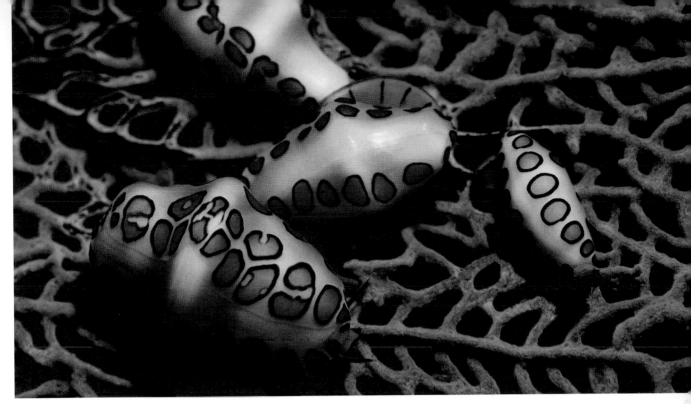

THE COASTLINE

Tobago has extensive coral reefs that are home to some very colorful fish; many are favorites in aquariums all over the world. Grunts, triggerfish, parrotfish, and butterfly fish are all quite common. Buccoo, situated in southwestern Tobago, is now a protected area, although tourism in past years caused much damage to fire and Staghorn coral, sea fans, and sea whips on the reef as well as many other species in the deeper waters.

Five species of turtle nest on the beaches of the islands. The largest is the leatherback, which can grow to 7 feet (2.1 m) and weigh 1,200 pounds (545 kilograms). Other species are the green turtle, loggerhead turtle, hawksbill turtle, and olive ridley, the smallest of the five. All of them share a common nesting habit of coming ashore to bury their eggs in the sand. Turtles are protected during the nesting season but are hunted at other times of the year.

On the shoreline, there are several very distinctive trees to be found. Almond and mango trees line the shores. This type of almond tree does not produce edible fruit. Coconut palms are also common, as are royal palms and traveler's palms.

CLIMATE

Trinidad and Tobago has a tropical climate of high relative humidity and distinct seasons, with a dry season between December and May and a wet season between June and November. During the wet season it rains for a short time in the late afternoon each day. June is the wettest month, while February is the driest month. During the dry season, temperatures tend to fall a little to an average of 79°F (26°C). April is the hottest month, with temperature highs of around 93.2°F (34°C).

The prevailing winds on the islands are northeast trade winds with a velocity of about 10 to 20 miles (16—22 km) per hour. They lower the temperature and bring rain to the eastern side of the islands.

Trinidad and Tobago is usually outside the hurricane zone. Hurricanes tend to form between June and September either in the north of the islands or in the eastern Atlantic Ocean near the Cape Verde islands, but occasionally the country is hit by a hurricane, notably in 1847, 1867, and 1963, when Hurricane Flora killed 7,000 people in the Caribbean.

Tropical Storm Alma hit Trinidad in 1974 as well, causing damage before obtaining full strength.

Water lilies near a lake in Trinidad. Most of the islands' plants have adapted to the tropical climate of the country.

URBAN CENTERS

The major urban center and capital of Trinidad and Tobago is Port-of-Spain, located on the west coast of Trinidad at the bottom of the peninsula that extends to the Dragon's Mouth passage in the Gulf of Paria. Port-of-Spain is also the chief port of the islands. The city lies on a coastal plain with hills to the east, which form the suburbs of the city. The old part of the city is now the business area and also houses government buildings. There are many well-laid-out parks, including a botanical garden. The largest airport in the Caribbean is 16 miles (26 km) outside the city at Piarco. Port-of-Spain's estimated official population is 51,076.

At the other end of the Gulf of Paria is Trinidad's second city, San Fernando. Like Port-of-Spain, it is an important shipping center and is located on a flat plain with the hills of the Central Range to the east. San Fernando is an administrative center for the south of the island, and was once the home of a community of Carib Indians. The city services the extensive oil fields of the south of the island. Its population is 55,419.

A typical day in the streets of Scarborough in Tobago.

Trinidad's third-largest and most newly developed town is Chaguanas, located halfway between San Fernando and Port-of-Spain. It is now an important business center servicing the oil industry, and like San Fernando and Arima, Chaguanas was once home to a group of Carib Indians. Arima, previously the third most important city in Trinidad, is now less vibrant, although it is still an important stop on the island's highway system.

The southern end of Trinidad is dominated by heavy industry, with several towns supporting the workers. Point Lisas is the major industrial center. Another urban center is Point-à-Pierre.

The main town in Tobago is Scarborough, which has a deep-water harbor on the Atlantic coast. The town sits on the steep sides of a hill overlooking Scarborough Harbor. It became the capital of the island in 1796, replacing Mount Saint George farther to the northeast. Scarborough has a population of 17,000, and is more rural than the towns of Trinidad. Most buildings, other than government ones or the few modern ones, are simple one-story structures with tin roofs. To the west of Scarborough is the international airport. The area around it has many tourist-oriented beach resorts and hotels with close access to the reefs at Buccoo.

BIRD OF PARADISE ISLAND

This island, sometimes known as Little Tobago, is situated about 1 mile (1.6 km) off the northeastern coast of Tobago, near a tiny village called Speyside. The island has been designated a wildlife sanctuary and is home to an introduced species of greater birds of paradise brought to the island in 1909 and much harmed by Hurricane Flora in 1963. The island is uninhabited by humans, but 58 species of birds live there.

Farther northeast along the coast is Roxborough, the second-largest settlement in Tobago. On the northern peninsula of the country lies Charlotteville. Charlotteville is slightly bigger than a village and is isolated by the surrounding mountains. The chief occupation there is fishing.

HISTORY

Stollmeyer's Castle is a historic house located in Port-of-Spain in Trinidad. This majestic landmark is part of a group of historic buildings known as the Magnificent Nine that are found in the area.

TRINIDAD IS PROBABLY THE FIRST island in the Caribbean to have been occupied by humans. Prior to 300 B.C., hunter-gatherer Meso-Indians lived on the island of Trinidad, leaving behind them stone tools and shell middens.

Shell middens, also known as kitchen middens, are used by archaeologists to describe a mound or deposit containing shells and other refuse. These middens contain man-made waste that is indicative of a previous human settlement.

Also known as the Carib stone, this Arawak petroglyph in Trinidad is believed by archaeologists to be at least 500 to 1,000 years old.

An artist's impression of Columbus and his crew arriving on an island. Columbus explored Trinidad in August 1498 before sighting and naming Tobago *Bella Forma*, or "beautiful form" in Spanish.

A second wave of settlers arrived on Tobago from South America around 300 B.C. These people were farmers who could make pots and cloth and who cultivated potatoes and cassava, which they used to make bread. They colonized most of the Lesser Antilles and spoke dialects of the Arawak language. However, around A.D. 1000, another group who spoke Carib dialects moved onto the islands.

The islands continued to be developed by these two groups of people for 500 years. It was their descendants whom Christopher Columbus met when he arrived on the island of Trinidad in 1498.

SPANISH COLONIALISM

The settlements that Columbus encountered were not permanent. People constantly moved to new areas of cultivation when the old areas became infertile. They lived in small village communities. Work was divided, with women doing domestic chores and the farming, while men did the hunting.

The Spanish did not settle in Trinidad for a century or so, though they raided it often for slaves. The first Spanish settlement was established in 1592 at Saint Joseph on Trinidad. For two centuries the Spanish colony survived, but with little investment from the Spanish Crown, and the town was regularly attacked by the British and Dutch. Missionaries arrived and established missions around the island. One mission was attacked by the Indians it sought to convert in 1699. Its missionaries, the governor, and several soldiers were killed.

Gradually settlers arrived and set up tobacco plantations, but these failed. Cocoa plantations were started later and were more successful until 1725, when the entire industry was wiped out by a crop disease. This was followed by smallpox in 1739, which killed many of the planters.

A FRENCH AND BRITISH COLONY

By 1777 Port-of-Spain was established as a small fort, with a church and about 80 thatched houses. With the other Caribbean islands having more to offer to settlers, it proved difficult to attract Spanish people to Trinidad, so the governor began to encourage French settlers who were Catholics. Any white immigrant was offered 130 acres (53 ha) for each family member who came, and 650 acres (263 ha) for each slave they brought.

Built in the 1770s, Fort George in Port-of-Spain sits on top of a hill overlooking the ocean.

Early Trinidadians and Tobagonians led hard lives, for in the 1700s most were working as slaves on the various plantations.

Trinidad became more French than Spanish as settlers from the other West Indian islands arrived. The French language was used, and the French tradition of Carnival was introduced. People of color or mixed ancestry were also attracted to the island by its lack of discrimination.

In 1790 slave trading was allowed on the island. Prior to this, slaves were brought in by their masters but were never bought and sold here. Cotton and sugar plantations began to thrive as slavery made cultivation possible.

Around this time Great Britain and France were at war, and the fighting often involved Trinidad, which was technically still a Spanish colony. In 1797 Trinidad was invaded by the British, and the Spanish surrendered. The Spanish were offered friendly terms of surrender, but the governor who was left in charge of the island treated the residents cruelly, particularly anyone he feared might be planning rebellion. Many people of color were imprisoned and tortured. This cruel rule lasted six years until the governor was replaced. In the same year, 1803, Tobago was invaded by the British. Trinidad subsequently became a Crown colony, ruled directly by Britain and administered by a governor.

THE SLAVE TRADE

Trinidad's development had been hindered by the restrictions on slave trading, which had lasted till 1790. By the time of British rule, abolitionists had begun to lobby the British government to restrict the slave trade in Trinidad. Other West Indian islands had already developed slave economies, and the abolitionists wished to stop another slave economy from developing in Trinidad. The other West Indian colonies agreed, because if Trinidad could not develop its sugar and cotton industries, there would be less competition for them. In 1806 the slave trade was forbidden to Trinidad and Tobago, although slaves already on the island were not freed. In 1812 the British issued an order that all slaves in Trinidad should be registered, and no more slaves could be used on the island beyond those registered. The order was ignored, and illegal slave trading continued.

Slaves being shipped to be traded overseas. The illlegal trading of natives continued despite the government's orders.

POSTSLAVERY

The repercussions of the injustice of slavery continued in Trinidad for years after abolition. The former slaves rebelled against working for their masters, and slavery was brought to an end in 1838, two years earlier than the legislation demanded. The former slaves now found themselves in a strong bargaining position. They could negotiate for good wages because there had always been a shortage of slaves, unlike in other West Indian colonies where even after freedom, former slaves still lived in poverty because there were too many of them to bargain for better wages. Some former slaves on Trinidad took up farm work on the plantations, some others moved to the cities and found work, and still others bought a small holding or squatted on unused land. In 1869 the squatters were allowed to buy their plots of land at a cost of 1 pound per 5 acres (2 ha).

Meanwhile the sugar and cotton plantations were suffering from a shortage of labor. Recruitment was attempted to attract American blacks, the Chinese on Madeira, and liberated slaves from other colonies, but those who came generally found work in the cities or bought their own small holding. In 1848 the British government began to encourage indentured laborers. In exchange for their passage, laborers from India had to work for the landowner for a certain number of years. The arrangement continued until 1917. When their period of indenture ended, the Indians followed the example of the former slaves and also bought plots of land. Thus more indentured laborers had to be brought from India, leading to modern Trinidad's ethnic mix.

TOBAGO

Tobago had a more difficult time. Up until 1803 the island changed hands many times among the French, Dutch, English, and Spanish, often suffering badly at each exchange of ruler. A slave economy emerged based on the cultivation of sugar and cotton, and although liberal legislation was passed allowing slaves to own land and providing allowances for their well-being, a slave rebellion was uncovered in 1801 just before it was to take place.

INDENTURED WORKERS

Once slavery was abolished on the islands, Great Britain turned to India, a country where conditions were so poor that people were willing to leave their country to work. These Indians were largely men who were indentured for five years to a plantation owner. After that they could choose to be indentured again or to do other work as long as they could pay a special tax. After five more years they were allowed free passage back to India. If the laborer broke his contract, it was a criminal offense and he would be imprisoned.

Conditions were harsh, pay was low, and there were few women with whom to make marriages. Unhappiness stalked their domestic life as well. Between 1872 and 1900, 87 Indian wives of indentured workers were murdered, mainly by their husbands because of their infidelities with other indentured workers. The Indians were despised in society. Nevertheless, after the indenture was over, few returned to India because their connections were now severed. Most stayed to become farmworkers or moved to the towns where they took up other trades.

Six rebel leaders were executed, and many more were flogged and banished. Emancipation came to Tobago at the same time as to the other colonies. Because Tobago had become more of a slave economy than Trinidad, it suffered more as a result. As in Trinidad, immigration was encouraged, but unlike in Trinidad, the wages were so low that few people could be persuaded to come. In 1847 a hurricane destroyed many plantations, and the falling price of sugar increased Tobago's distress. For a few years a system where farm workers shared the crops with the landowner seemed to work, but eventually the landowners were making so little money that the scheme fell through. In 1889 Tobago was made a ward of Trinidad, and the two islands were legally one country for the first time.

By 1900 Port-of-Spain was a major urban center, and a quarter of the population lived there. Huge numbers of disenfranchised urban poor lived beside the rich, white French and English settlers. In 1903 there was a riot in Port-of-Spain over water shortages. Eighteen people were killed, and the government building was burned down. Although the riots were about water, they were taken to be an indication of political unrest, and plans began to instate a representative assembly in Trinidad. In 1913 the assembly was installed with a very limited franchise.

AN OIL ECONOMY

The world's first oil well was sunk in 1857 at La Brea in southern Trinidad, long before the internal combustion engine would provide a sufficient incentive for the drillers. Oil burning engines became commercially viable in the 1890s, and Trinidad's economy changed forever. When the British navy began to buy diesel-powered ships, British money and engineering skills poured into Trinidad. During the pioneering days of the oil industry, there were many accidents, but by 1929 the technology had been developed.

RACE RELATIONS

During World War I, life became very hard for working men in Trinidad, and there was a lot of political unrest and strikes. The black men who volunteered to fight for Great Britain were banned from killing Germans for fear that they might get used to killing white men. They were kept in segregated units and commanded by white officers. In the months following the end of the war, the West Indian troops were sent to Italy to act as domestic servants to the white troops. Several rebelled and were imprisoned. The returning soldiers told stories of racial discrimination, rapidly followed by news of anti-black demonstrations in Great Britain. The victory celebrations in Trinidad were boycotted, and white businessmen began to feel threatened. In 1919 black dockworkers held a strike for better pay. When they were refused, they walked away from their jobs. When non-union labor was brought in, warehouses were smashed. Workers throughout Trinidad joined in the disturbances. British troops intervened, and leading strikers were arrested and imprisoned. Strikes were made illegal, and newspapers and radical publications were banned.

In 1925 the franchise was extended, and Indians and trade union representatives were elected to the legislature. But as the worldwide

The Trinidadian Memorial Park, where war heroes are commemorated.

depression began to hit Trinidad, workers grew poorer, and people began to suffer from hunger. In 1934 hunger marches were organized around the island. In 1937 oil workers began a sit-down strike and were chased away by the police. Two oil wells were set on fire. When police tried to arrest the leader, a crowd attacked them, and two policemen were killed. The strikes spread to other oil fields and other industries, and it began to look like a revolution. British warships were sent to Trinidad, and the strikes fizzled out. Some concessions to the workers' demands were made, and the threat of revolution disappeared. However, the unions had grown strong and remained a threat to employers right up to World War II.

POSTWAR POLITICS

After the war political groups and individuals with different platforms competed for seats in the legislature. By the 1956 election, there were seven parties and 39 independents. The parties represented different social and ethnic groups; the strongest was the PNM (People's Nationalist Movement), a black nationalist party. The next most powerful group was the PDP (People's

WORLD WAR II

When World War II began, part of Trinidad was leased to the United States, and huge military bases were built. Warships filled the Gulf of Paria and were hunted by German U-boats. Things improved for Trinidadians: There was high employment, along with better wages and a roaring nightlife that catered to the American troops. The war came to an end in May 1945. Shortly afterward constitutional reforms provided for universal suffrage.

Democratic Party). The PNM formed the government, and the process toward independence began in 1962. The two parties predominated in the islands: the PNM, made up of black nationalists intellectuals with the support of the trade unions, who wanted to take back the oil fields that had been leased to the United States by Great Britain; and the PDP, largely white and Indian, unionist, and in favor of international capital. In the 1961 election, white and Indian homes and businesses were looted. On the verge of a serious racial war, Trinidadians and Tobagonians went to the polls and gave the PNM a large majority. The following year, Trinidad and Tobago became an independent state under the leadership of Eric Williams.

A resurgent Jamaat al Muslimeen continues to be a threat to stability in Trinidad and Tobago.

INDEPENDENCE

Although the PNM campaigned against foreign capital and supported trade unions when seeking power, it changed its stance once in control, inviting foreign investment and reducing the power of the trade unions. The opposition PDP faded into the background, and the islands became virtually a one-party state. After a series of strikes for better pay, the Industrial Stabilization Act was passed in 1965, making strikes impossible.

Despite rising oil revenues, things did not improve for the black majority in Trinidad. The educational system did improve their quality of training, but there were no jobs for young blacks. With the banning of strikes and no prospect of improvement, a black power movement developed. Workers began to organize strikes in contravention of the law. In 1970 there were black power demonstrations in Port-of-Spain.

Williams died in 1981 while still holding office. The PNM remained in power following the death of Williams, but its 30-year rule ended in 1986 when the National Alliance for Reconstruction (NAR), a multiethnic coalition aimed at uniting Trinidadians of Afro-Trinidadian and Indo-Trinidadian descent, won a landslide victory by capturing 33 of 36 seats. Tobago's A.N.R. Robinson, the political leader of the NAR, was named prime minister.

In July 1990 the Jamaat al Muslimeen, an extremist Black Muslim group with an unresolved grievance against the government over land claims, tried to overthrow the NAR government. The group held the prime minister and members of parliament hostage for five days, while rioting shook Port-of-Spain. After a long standoff with the police and military, the Jamaat al Muslimeen leader, Yasin Abu Bakr, and his followers surrendered to Trinidadian authorities.

In the most recent elections held on May 24, 2010, the People's Partnership, a coalition of parties, won 29 out of 41 seats. As a result of the People's Partnership's win, Kamla Persad-Bissessar of the People's Partnership coalition was elected Trinidad and Tobago's first female prime minister.

Armed police during the 1970 demonstration. A state of emergency was declared in response to the demonstration. A movement called the United Labor Front was also formed as a result of the incident.

The FBI recently opened an office in Trinidad in connection with its hunt for a terrorist.

GOVERNMENT

Soldiers standing guard outside an important
international conference in Port-of-Spain in Trinidad.

CHAPTER 3

TRINIDAD AND TOBAGO FIRST acquired a common government in 1889. Prior to that Tobago was a British colony that was not related to its larger neighbor.

It had a bicameral legislature, while Trinidad had a simpler, single legislative assembly. The merger of the two countries meant that the government of Tobago shifted to Trinidad, although Tobago retained separate taxes and a smaller subordinate legislature.

In 1925 the national legislature was reformed and members added. This was followed by a universal suffrage in 1945. Government rule was carried out by a party-based cabinet, but authority was based in Great Britain.

The White Hall is a distinct symbol of the country's independence.

The iconic legislative parliament building in Trinidad.

INDEPENDENCE

Independence occurred in 1962, although the links with Great Britain were not completely severed. The islands then became part of the British Commonwealth and were to be ruled by a governor general who was not elected, but appointed by Britain. The governor had a cabinet made up of elected representatives. Beneath the cabinet was a bicameral legislature, along the lines of the American system. Both the houses were elected.

In 1976 the current constitution was adopted. This removed the governor general and instituted a non-executive president heading a republic. The president, currently George Maxwell Richards, is elected by an electoral college of all the country's ministers. Below the president is a cabinet chosen by and headed by the prime minister. The prime minister and cabinet are responsible to parliament.

The legislature, or parliament, consists of two houses—one of them is the House of Representatives with 41 members who are directly elected. Legislation originates and passes from this house to the Senate, which is made up of 31 members appointed by the president. Sixteen of these are chosen on the advice of the prime minister, six on the recommendation of the leader of the opposition, and nine by the president, from among outstanding members of the community. Elections to the House of Representatives are held every five years.

Tobago has its own devolved House of Assembly, set up in 1980, which can legislate on some financial matters and other local issues such as urban and rural development, education, health, and housing. It has 12 elected members. In the most recent elections in Tobago, held on January 19, 2009, PNM won eight seats, while a new party the Tobago Organization of the People won four seats.

POLITICAL PARTIES

For several years after independence, Trinidad and Tobago had a chaotic electoral system with individuals competing for seats in parliament. Eventually a series of political parties formed, mostly along racial lines. The first parties to form before independence were PNM and PDP; both were formed in the 1950s. The PNM contested the elections of 1956 along with seven other parties. The PNM represented the black middle classes and stood for better education and nationalism, and strongly criticized the ruling white

Voters wait in line in Carapo, Trinidad and Tobago, during the May 2010 elections.

The new prime minister of Trinidad and Tobago, Kamla Persad-Bissessar (*right*) beams next to President Maxwell Richards (*left*) after being sworn in. A lawyer, she is the first woman to hold the position.

elite. The PNM won majorities in most elections from 1956 until 1986, and so the government of Trinidad was in the hands of a party that represented black middle-class interests.

The PDP was largely Indian in makeup and for many years formed the chief opposition party. In the 1970s the PDP merged with a radical group, the Action Committee of Dedicated Citizens (ACDC), and became the Democratic Liberation Party (DLP).

In Tobago the PNM did less well and a series of coalitions led by the politician Arthur Napoleon Raymond Robinson took control of the assembly.

In 1986 the PNM lost power in Trinidad as a coalition of very diverse parties representing big business, trade unions, rural Indians, and all Tobagonians called the Alliance for National Reconstruction (ANR) took power. For the first time the country was led by a multiethnic party, but it did not last because the measures that were necessary at the time proved too unpleasant for the electorate. After a coup the coalition collapsed and the PNM returned to power in 1991.

The 1995 election saw the emergence of another single-race party, the United National Congress (UNC). Seats in the House of Representatives were split exactly between the two parties, the PNM and the UNC, with two ANR members supporting the UNC. For the first time in Trinidad's history there was an Indian prime minister, Basdeo Panday.

Kamla Persad-Bissessar is the seventh and current prime minister of the Republic of Trinidad and Tobago. She was sworn in as the country's first female prime minister on May 26, 2010.

THE JUDICIAL SYSTEM

Trinidad and Tobago's judicial system is based on the British legal system. The highest court is the Supreme Court, which consists of a High Court and a Court of Appeal. Presently the final court of appeal for Trinidadians is the Privy Council in London, but provision is being made for a Caribbean Supreme Court, which would replace the function of the Privy Council. However, the government has been unable to pass legislation to bring about this change. Trinidad and Tobago is also the seat of the Caribbean Court of Justice (CCJ), which was inaugurated on April 16, 2005. The CCJ is intended to replace the Privy Council as the final Court of Appeal for the member states of the Caribbean Community and Common Market (CARICOM). Since its inauguration only two states, Barbados and Guyana, have acceded to the authority of the CCJ.

Below the higher courts there is a system of magistrate courts to deal with less important matters. Trinidad and Tobago has 16 judges appointed by the president based on the advice given by the legal service commission. The chief justice is also appointed by the president on the advice of the prime minister. All primary posts in the judicial system are filled at the discretion of the president and prime minister.

The district court in Port-of-Spain.

REGIONAL POLITICS

In April 2006 the Permanent Court of Arbitration issued a decision that set up a maritime boundary between Trinidad and Tobago and Barbados, and

In 1996 a gang of nine men murdered a family in the southern Williamsville, Trinidad. Found guilty of the murder, the nine men were sentenced to death, a mandatory punishment under Trinidad and Tobago law. The men's lawyers took their case to the Privy Council in London in May 1999. But more than the lives of these nine men was resting on the Privy Council's decision.

Tension was high among the Caribbean countries, many of which also use the British Privy Council as a last court of appeal, since the sovereign rights of Trinidad and Tobago would be challenged if the Privy Council commuted the sentence. The Privy Council upheld the conviction, and the nine men were executed in June 1999, despite pleas for mercy by Archbishop Desmond Tutu and other international figures. The nine men were all drug racketeers, and 80 percent of public opinion in Trinidad supported the death penalty.

The decision of the Privy Council ensured that men on death rows all over the Caribbean would now face the death penalty. In June 1999 there were at least 100 men on death row in Trinidad alone.

During 2000 Trinidad and Tobago had the dubious global distinction of holding and executing the highest number of prisoners on death row.

compelled Barbados to enter a fishing agreement that limited Barbadian fishermen's catches of flying fish in Trinidad and Tobago's exclusive economic zone. Trinidad and Tobago has taken a leading role in the CARICOM as it is the most industrialized and second-largest country in the English-speaking Caribbean. CARICOM members are working to establish a Single Market and Economy (CSME).

Trinidad is a member of the Organization of American States and has signed a treaty with the United States on cooperation over international crime. About 90 percent of Trinidadian crime is drug-related.

SOME POLITICAL FIGURES

The most important political figure and charismatic leader in Trinidad and Tobago was Eric Williams, but there are many other important people who have played a part in Trinidad and Tobago's political life. Bhadase Maharaj was the president of Maha Sabha, an orthodox Hindu association. He took an active part in politics, for a time leading the PDP. He represented the Indian equivalent of Williams but was never able to mobilize Indian Muslims to his side. He was a flamboyant character and often carried guns in public. He was succeeded as leader of DLP in 1960 by Rudranath Capildeo, another Indian, this time from an academic background. In the 1961 election he recommended that people arm themselves against the PNM and prepare to take over the country. The DLP lost that election, even in Tobago.

Basdeo Panday was a young lawyer in 1971 when he became interested in politics and was persuaded to lead a party called the United Liberation Front (ULF), a combination of several other small parties, including the DLP. In 1995 he became Trinidad's first ethnic Indian prime minister. President Panday is a Tobagonian who has taken an active part in the country's politics for many years. His party, another coalition, took power in 1986, and in July 1990 President Robinson was taken hostage by a small, radical Muslim group for 6 days during a coup.

The previous president of Trinidad and Tobago, Arthur Robinson (*left*), poses with previous U.S. president Jimmy Carter and Rosalynn Carter during a meeting in Atlanta.

ECONOMY

People cross the road near a branch of the Royal Bank of Trinidad and Tobago (RBTT) in Port-of-Spain.

CHAPTER 4

T
RINIDAD AND TOBAGO HAS A mixed economy with some areas of the economy being owned and run by the state, while the majority are run by private enterprise.

Trinidad and Tobago has earned a reputation as an excellent investment site for international businesses, and has one of the highest growth rates and per capita incomes in Latin America. Recent growth has been fueled by investments in liquefied natural gas (LNG), petrochemicals, and steel. Additional petrochemical, aluminum, and plastics projects are in various stages of planning. The country is also a regional financial center, and tourism is a growing sector, although it is not proportionately as important as in many other Caribbean islands. The economy benefits from a growing trade surplus. The currency is the Trinidad and Tobago dollar. It is now pegged with the U.S. dollar, with one U.S dollar equaling $6.25 in Trinidad and Tobago dollars.

Cargo being loaded and unloaded at the port in Trinidad.

A water-taxi service between San Fernando and Port-of-Spain has been started to ease the congestion and entice more commuters to leave their cars at home.

Oil and gas account
for about 40
percent of GDP, but
only 5 percent
of employment.

THE OIL AND GAS INDUSTRY

Oil was discovered in Trinidad in 1857 when the world's first oil well was drilled at La Brea. In 1914 the first oil refinery was built in Trinidad and Tobago at Point-à-Pierre. By 1946 Trinidadian oil represented 65 percent of the British Empire's oil production. A second refinery has been added recently at Point Fortin. For the last 25 years oil has dominated the country's economy.

There are 30 operating oil and gas fields, mostly in the south of Trinidad or off the southwestern coast. Current reserves of oil are thought to be about 793 million barrels. In 1997 further exploration began, and the government sold off six areas for exploration, retaining a 50 percent interest. There has been a 30 percent increase in oil production since 2003, but production has remained fairly constant since 2008. The oil and gas industry employs about 61,500 people.

Natural gas is another important sector of Trinidad and Tobago's economy. Reserves have declined from 18 trillion cubic feet (510 cubic km)

Trinidad is a producer of methanol. The plants around the country produce about a tenth of the world's methanol.

to 16.74 trillion cubic feet (474 cubic km). The gas is turned into liquefied natural gas, and about 3.9 billion cubic feet (0.11 cubic km) is produced a day. By 2016 natural gas production is estimated to increase to 5.9 billion cubic feet (0.17 cubic km) a day. The government is encouraging energy companies to pursue an aggressive exploratory program in deep water, as well as on land and near shore areas to ensure that new supplies of gas are found to meet the huge gas demand.

HEAVY INDUSTRY

Several industries have emerged as a result of the development of the oil industry. A petrochemical industry produces by-products of oil for export and local use. Trinidad and Tobago is currently the world's largest producer of ammonia and methanol, and provides over 70 percent of all liquefied natural gas (LNG) and methanol imports to the United States.

Other major industries include car assembly, radio and television production, paper products and printing, cement, furniture, processed food, and clothes.

The scale and sophistication of the car industry provides skilled employment in the job market.

AGRICULTURE

From being a major producer of coffee, sugar, and cocoa in the last century, Trinidad and Tobago has developed a more industrialized economy. Agriculture now accounts for about 0.5 percent of GDP and employs a small percentage of the population. About 14.62 percent of the land is arable, and 9.16 percent of the land is used for permanent crops.

There are two distinct types of agricultural operations—the large estate or plantation that is managed by a specialist and employs large numbers of laborers, and the small farm cultivated by the owner (or tenant) and family. The small farms grow mainly for the home market. Crops include corn, rice, peas, beans, potatoes, other vegetables, and a wide variety of

Trinidad is also home to the world's largest methanol production plant.

fruits. Lowland rice is grown almost entirely by Indian farmers. The large estates are interested mainly in commercial export crops, although the small farmers also grow some export crops. The value of crops grown for the domestic market is believed to be considerably greater than that of the export crops. In January 2007 plans were announced to close the centuries-old sugar industry, which had been badly hit by cuts in subsidies from the European Union. Before that, in August 2003, the state-owned sugar company Caroni had shut down with the loss of more than 8,000 jobs. The major export crop, cocoa, is cultivated in the hill sections of both Trinidad and Tobago. Estates produce considerably more cocoa than small holdings, owing to better agricultural practices and to the fact that small farmers intercrop bananas, coffee, and other crops with cocoa. Livestock farming is also a local business. It is estimated that the islands have about 30,000 cattle, 28,366 pigs, and 8,469 sheep, all owned by small farmers for sale in local markets. Chickens are also an important staple, and buffalo are kept mainly for transportation and for plowing fields.

Fiery-colored cacao seed pods growing on a plantation in Trinidad and Tobago.

TRANSPORTATION

Trinidad's main transportation system is its network of roads. The islands have 5,170 miles (8,320 km) of roads, but congestion and pollution are increasing. Freight is transported by road in trucks. The main air route into Trinidad is via Piarco International Airport, and the chief ports are Port-of-Spain, Point Fortin, Point-à-Pierre, and Scarborough, as well as Point Lisas, the main industrial complex in the country.

TOURISM

Tourism is a growing sector in Trinidad and Tobago, although it is not financially as important as in many other Caribbean islands. Tourism is centered on the less industrially developed Tobago, with most of the beach resorts and tourist hotels concentrated there. It is served by an airport capable of taking wide-bodied aircraft, and there are plans to develop a third international airport on Trinidad. Port-of-Spain on Trinidad is a major tourist destination, and most cruise ships enter the islands at Port-of-Spain Harbor. Scarborough in Tobago is another destination for tourist ships. The islands are less dependent on tourism than other Caribbean islands and so are not so susceptible to the disadvantages of the industry—cluttered beaches and damaged environment caused by inconsiderate tourists, tour buses, and excessive development of infrastructure.

Tourists snorkel in turquoise blue Caribbean waters from a glass-bottom excursion boat anchored off the coast of Tobago. Tourists are attracted by the well-conserved natural beauty of the country.

There are now half a million private cars on the road in Trinidad and Tobago, and congestion has reached epidemic levels. The traffic jam starts before 6:00 A.M., and chokes movement into and out of Port-of-Spain.

Many businesses have difficulty operating properly, since employees as well as owners often arrive later than scheduled opening times, mainly due to uncontrollable traffic and transportation issues. Workers are leaving their homes at least 45 minutes earlier just to get to work, and they spend an average of 45 minutes to an hour in traffic either way.

Trinidad once had a railway line, but it was closed down in the mid-20th century. On April 11, 2008, the Trinitrain Consortium announced that it would plan and build a 65.2-mile (105-km) two-line Trinidad Rapid Railway. The new railways are needed urgently to overcome crippling road congestion.

THE FISHING INDUSTRY

The fishing industry has great potential, but current production does not begin to meet local demands, and large quantities of fish must be imported.

In 1977 the government offered financial incentives to people prepared to take up the livelihood. It has been estimated that 13,000 people are involved in the industry, with 50,000 people being indirectly involved. Unfortunately the area around the islands has become overfished, and Trinidad often finds itself in dispute with neighboring Venezuela over territorial rights. The job of the navy is to patrol the waters for rogue fishermen. Trinidadians are also sometimes caught fishing illegally in Venezuelan waters. Trinidad allows the use of ghost nets—transparent plastic nets—that are banned by many other countries because of the effect they have on fish stocks. Trinidad has had a shrimp fleet since the 1970s. The shrimp is canned and processed on the island.

Starting in the 1970s ghost nets grew to staggering sizes, many spanning as much as 10 to 30 miles (16.1-48.3 km) in length. Designed to surround anything that swims into them—and make it impossible to escape—the nets fail to discriminate between the fish being sought and all other marine life.

Fishermen stretching out their nets in Tobago.

ENVIRONMENT

A starfish is washed up on the sandy
shores of Pigeon Point in Tobago.

THE ENVIRONMENT OF TRINIDAD and Tobago reflects the interaction between its biodiversity, high population density, and industrialized economy. Environmental issues include water pollution from agricultural chemicals, industrial wastes, and raw sewage; oil pollution of beaches; deforestation; and soil erosion.

The rocky coastal landscape in Trinidad and Tobago.

An interesting phenomenon is the widespread use of the flora of the islands, including medicinal plants to treat diabetes. Some pet owners even use medicinal plants to treat their dogs for diarrhea or to get rid of parasites.

The Naviva Swamp is one of the protected areas in Trinidad and Tobago.

MARINE POLLUTION

One major area of concern in Trinidad and Tobago is marine pollution. Various substances enter streams, rivers, wetlands, and the surrounding oceans. With population growth, tourism, and business development, pollution is increasing, and in some areas, raw sewage ends up in the rivers and surrounding oceans via various sources of drainage. Industry also contributes to oil pollution, water treatment wastes, solid wastes, and pesticides and fertilizers, which alter water temperatures, and in some cases, are related to reef degradation. Furthermore many pollutants cause oxygen depletion in the water, resulting in the death of certain marine organisms.

Pollutants have also been known to clog fish gills, causing significant fish kills, as documented in the Gulf of Paria. Mangrove swamps and wetlands are also affected as a vital part of the marine system; they provide breeding grounds for many fish and shellfish. When they are polluted, the fish and shellfish end up being unable to breed and their population drops.

AIR POLLUTION

Trinidad and Tobago is rated eleventh in the world for carbon dioxide emissions per capita. Carbon dioxide is one of the primary greenhouse gases that contribute to global warming. Although Trinidad and Tobago's national output of greenhouse gases is high, the primary source is heavy industrial processes and not the general population. On an individual basis, residential emissions are about one-tenth of those produced by countries such as the United States and Canada. Still emissions in the region are high, and may be a contributor to higher incidences of respiratory illness.

CONSERVATION ORGANIZATIONS

In March 1995 the Environmental Management Authority (EMA) in Trinidad and Tobago was established. Start-up funding for the institution was made available through a World Bank loan with additional assistance from the United Nations Development Programme (UNDP) and the government of Trinidad and Tobago. The authority began operations in June 1995 and now facilitates cooperation among NGOs and community-based organizations. The EMA is mandated to write and enforce laws as well as to conserve natural resources. In 2003 the EMA succeeded in converting the nation to unleaded gasoline, which helped lower greenhouse gas emissions. By 2020 the Trinidad and Tobago government hopes to achieve environmental sustainability and bring Trinidad and Tobago the status of "developed nation."

RECYCLING

In the 2009 budget statement, the government of Trinidad and Tobago announced that it had decided to focus on a general waste recycling system. The Trinidad and Tobago government sought the assistance of the Canadian province of Nova Scotia to draft legislation for the new system, which would create a new independent statutory waste authority under the wing of the Ministry of Local Government, empower the waste authority to issue regulations on creating a deposit-return system for several streams of recyclables, and provide for the creation of a nationwide system of collection depots for recyclables.

The delicate balance of nature is held together by all aspects of natural life, such as this tufted coquette keeping flight while feeding at a flower in Trinidad.

WASTE TREATMENT AND DISPOSAL

A sign on a tree in Tobago reminds visitors not to litter.

Trinidad and Tobago is well on track to achieve the United Nations Millennium Development Goal (MDG) of ensuring environmental sustainability and adequate access to safe drinking water and sanitation facilities for its 1.3 million people by 2015. Although it comes at varying levels of service, 92 percent of the population already has access to drinking water, and about 92 percent of the population has sanitation coverage through a diverse range of waste disposal systems. The mandate given by the government to the state-owned Water and Sewerage Authority (WASA) is to upgrade the water and sanitation sectors at all levels in the shortest time possible. Trinidad and Tobago also has implemented a US$200 million program to improve water and wastewater service delivery.

FLORA AND FAUNA

The flora of Trinidad and Tobago is believed to include about 2,500 species. There are about 50 species of freshwater fish (plus 30 marine species that are occasionally found in freshwater), 400 to 500 species of marine fish, 30 species of amphibians, and about species of 90 reptiles.

TRINIDAD PIPING-GUAN The Trinidad piping-guan is a bird species found only on Trinidad and is close to extinction. It is a large bird, 23.6 inches (60 cm) in length, and similar in general appearance to a turkey, with a thin neck and small head. Trinidad piping-guans are forest birds, and they build their nests in trees. The female lays three large white eggs and she incubates them alone. This arboreal species feeds on fruit and berries.

The Trinidad piping-guan is mainly black with a purple gloss. Its large crest is blackish, edged with white, and it has large white wing patches. The bare face and wattle are blue, and the legs are red. Its call is a thin piping. The wings make a whirring sound in flight.

WEST INDIAN MANATEE The West Indian manatee has adapted fully to an aquatic lifestyle, having no hind limbs. The average West Indian manatee is about 9.8 feet (3 m) long, and weighs between 880 and 1,320 pounds (400 and 600 kg), with females generally being larger than males. The largest individuals can weigh up to 3,300 pounds (1,500 kg) and measure up to 15 feet (4.6 m). As its name implies the West Indian manatee lives in the West Indies, or Caribbean, generally in shallow coastal areas. However, it is known to withstand large changes in water salinity, and so has also been found in shallow rivers and estuaries. It is limited to the tropics and subtropics due to an extremely low metabolic rate and lack of a thick layer of blubber—the insulating body fat. During summer these large mammals have even been found as far north as New York City. The West Indian manatee is surprisingly agile in water, and individuals have been seen doing rolls, somersaults, and even swimming upside-down.

Large adult manatees feast on nearly 20 to 66 pounds (9 to 30 kg) of sea grasses and plant leaves daily. Because manatees feed on abrasive plants, their molars are often worn down and are continually replaced throughout life.

Trinidad piping-guans on a branch in Trinidad.

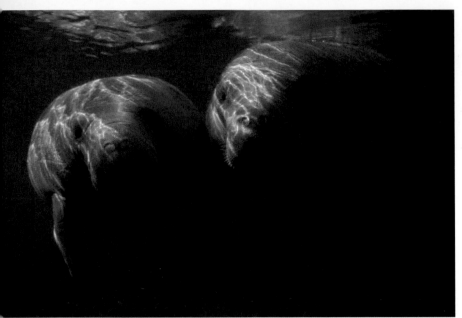

The West Indian manatee has been hunted for hundreds of years for its meat and hide, and continues to be hunted to this day. Illegal poaching, as well as collisions with speeding motorboats, is a constant source of manatee fatalities. Due to the manatee's low reproductive rate, a decline in manatee population may be hard to overcome.

West Indian manatees are protected in Trinidad and Tobago.

In 1992, following the success of Nature Seekers in Matura, the Grande Riviere Environmental Awareness Trust (GREAT) was established with the aim of protecting nesting leatherback turtles on Grande Riviere beach.

LEATHERBACK SEA TURTLE

The leatherback sea turtle is the largest of all living sea turtles and the fourth-largest modern reptile behind three crocodilians. It can easily be differentiated from other modern sea turtles by its lack of a bony shell. Instead its carapace—the bony case covering the back of an animal—is covered by skin and oily flesh.

The leatherback sea turtle is critically endangered around the world for numerous reasons. People around the world still harvest sea turtle eggs. Asian exploitation of turtle nests has been cited as the most significant factor for the species' global population decline. In Southeast Asia, egg harvesting in countries such as Thailand and Malaysia has led to a near-total collapse of local nesting populations. In the Caribbean some cultures consider the eggs to be aphrodisiacs. As an ocean species, the leatherback is occasionally caught as bycatch, that is, caught unintentionally due to commercial methods of fishing. Because these are the largest living sea turtles, turtle excluder devices can be ineffective with mature adults. It is reported that an average of 1,500 mature females were accidentally caught annually in the 1990s. Pollution, both chemical and physical, can also be fatal. Many turtles die from malabsorption and intestinal blockage following the ingestion of balloons and plastic bags that resemble their jellyfish prey. Chemical pollution also has an adverse effect on the leatherbacks.

NATURE SEEKERS

Nature Seekers is a community-based organization formed in 1990 to protect nesting leatherback turtles in Trinidad and Tobago. The group's main conservation efforts are based around providing tour guide services to visitors of Matura Beach, tagging turtles for tracking, and patrolling the beach to protect the turtles and their nests, although the group is also concerned with reforestation and keeping the beach clean. In addition to being instrumental in efforts toward protecting Trinidad's leatherback turtles, the group has demonstrated the importance of community involvement in the efforts, and has strengthened the ecotourism industry in Trinidad.

Prior to the foundation of Nature Seekers, the killing of female leatherback turtles by poachers had become such a serious problem that in 1990 Matura Beach was declared a prohibited area under the Forest Act. In order to find a long-term solution to this problem, the Wildlife Section of the Forestry Division worked together with the Matura community to establish a tour-guide training program. The intent of this program was to educate the community about the need to protect the turtles and their nests, and it was from this program that Nature Seekers was formed. Although initially Nature Seekers operated purely on a volunteer basis, and had great difficulty obtaining funds, it was later commissioned by the government to patrol the beach and to provide a mandatory tour-guide service to visitors. Although Nature Seekers has remained a nongovernmental organization (NGO), it has frequently worked in cooperation with the government to protect leatherback turtles.

The main project of Nature Seekers is the Matura Turtle Conservation Programme, which is also the first project that was begun with the foundation of the organization. This project consists of several smaller programs aimed at the protection of leatherback turtles in Trinidad. One of these programs involves patrolling the beach in order to protect the turtles from poachers and assist with the nesting process, as well as providing tour-guide services to visitors in order to promote greater awareness of the necessity of conservation. In addition to tours of the beach, Nature Seekers conducts tours of several other natural attractions in the area.

Another important project under the Matura Turtle Conservation Programme is the Pilot Sea Turtle Tagging Project, which is carried out in association with the Forestry Division, the Wider Caribbean Sea Turtle Network (WIDECAST), and the Institute of Marine Affairs. This project involves tagging sea turtles to track their migration patterns and gathering data from hatched nests.

The Matura Turtle Conservation Programme also consists of an annual effort to clean up Matura Beach and a study of ways to reduce the impact of tourism on turtles and their nests. Both are part of an effort by Nature Seekers to make Matura Beach a suitable place for both the turtles and visitors. Nature Seekers also runs an Adopt a Turtle program, which provides funds for other projects and educates participants about the turtles they adopt.

Besides the Matura Turtle Conservation Programme, Nature Seekers also participates in the National Reforestation and Watershed Rehabilitation Programme. The organization manages one of 55 projects in Trinidad as part of this program, which involves reforestation and the development of ecotourism activities that have a low impact on the environment.

At first there was much opposition in the Matura community toward the new conservation efforts. Many people made a living off of turtle meat and eggs, and they were worried that the restrictions would interfere with their ability to survive. Even more people resented the beach being closed off during turtle nesting season, because many locals used the beach for recreation. However, over time, Nature Seekers has had a positive effect on the community. In addition to creating jobs within the organization, the increased tourism brought to Matura by Nature Seekers created a strong tourism industry in the village, with many villagers operating bed and breakfasts and other tourism-related businesses. Nature Seekers has also been successful in generating community awareness about the importance of conservation. Even some poachers and their families have become convinced of the importance of conservation, and some have even joined Nature Seekers. Nature Seekers claims to have brought down the rate of turtles being slaughtered from 30 percent to zero. Because of the effectiveness of the conservation efforts, Nature Seekers has become a model for similar programs in other parts of Trinidad.

In 2006 Nature Seekers joined other community organizations as well as the Forestry Division and BHP Billiton Petroleum Trinidad & Tobago to form an organization called Turtle Village Trust. The stated goal of the organization is to establish Trinidad and Tobago as "the Premier Turtle Tourism Destination." It plans to accomplish this goal by assisting in the formation of partnerships between conservation groups and local communities, the like of which were responsible for the success of Nature Seekers in the Matura community. Nature Seekers has received numerous awards for their efforts in conservation and protecting Trinidad's leatherback turtles.

NATIONAL PARKS AND RESERVES IN TRINIDAD

ASA WRIGHT NATURE CENTER The Asa Wright Nature Center and Lodge is a nature resort and a scientific research station in the Arima Valley of the Northern Range in Trinidad and Tobago. This center is one of the top birdwatching spots in the Caribbean. A total of 159 species of birds have been recorded there. The center is owned by a non-profit trust. The center recently acquired the Rapsey Estate in the Aripo Valley, just west of the Arima Valley.

CARONI SWAMP BIRD SANCTUARY The Caroni Swamp is an important tourist attraction and provides important habitat for the scarlet ibis, one of the national birds of Trinidad and Tobago.

A silky anteater in the Caroni Swamp of Trinidad and Tobago.

NARIVA SWAMP Four major wetland vegetation types occur in the Nariva Swamp—mangrove swamp forest, palm forest, swamp wood, and freshwater marsh. The Nariva Swamp is threatened by rice cultivation in the northwest and watermelon cultivation in the southwest. It has also been affected by channelization in the swamp and deforestation of its watershed.

POINTE-À-PIERRE WILDFOWL TRUST Founded in 1966, the Pointe-à-Pierre Wild Fowl Trust is a not-for-profit environmental non-government organization dedicated to environmental education and the conservation of wetlands and waterfowl. Located in Pointe-à-Pierre, Trinidad and Tobago, the trust contains two lakes and about 61.7 acres (25 hectares) within the Petrotrin Oil Refinery.

NATURAL PARKS AND RESERVES IN TOBAGO

BUCCOO REEF AND SPEYSIDE Tobago's fringing coral reefs are some of the best in the region, and because of the area's nutrient-rich coastal waters, the reefs are also home to an impressive abundance of marine life, ranging from the microscopic to the huge. Located close to the South American continent, Tobago is washed from the south by the Guyana Current, which carries nutrients from the Orinoco River. These nutrients produce an abundance of plankton, which often gives a green or brown tint to the surface waters during the rainy season (June to December). This plankton

The giant brain coral off Speyside. Like many species of coral, brain corals are in danger due to their slow growth rate and changes in their marine environment.

is the primary food for a thriving food web of marine life of all shapes and sizes. Much of it ends up as food for the massive shoals of small fry, which in turn feed large predatory fish, such as jacks, barracudas, wahoos, tarpons, and tuna. Other large animals that are frequently seen include sea turtles, reef sharks, hammerhead sharks, groupers, eagle rays, and manta rays. The rich waters are also the reason for the massive size of some of the hard corals such as the giant brain coral off Speyside, which is over 19.7 feet (6 m) wide, and the huge barrel sponges that can be seen in the Columbus Passage south of Tobago.

A red-billed tropicbird in Little Tobago. These birds breed on the islands, laying a single egg directly onto the ground or a cliff ledge.

MAIN RIDGE FOREST RESERVE The Tobago Forest Reserve (or the Main Ridge Reserve) claims to be the oldest protected forest in the Western world. It was designated as a protected British Crown reserve on April 17, 1776, following recommendations by Soame Jenyns, a member of Parliament in Great Britain who had the responsibility for the development of Tobago. It has remained a protected area ever since.

This forested area has great biodiversity, including many species of birds, mammals, frogs, nonpoisonous snakes, butterflies, and other invertebrates. It is one of the most approachable areas of rain forest, since it is relatively small and there are government-appointed guides who provide an authoritative guiding service through the forest at a reasonable cost.

LITTLE TOBAGO Little Tobago, the small neighboring island, supports some of the best dry forest remaining in Tobago. Little Tobago and Saint Giles Island are important seabird nesting colonies, with red-billed tropicbirds, magnificent frigatebirds and Audubon's shearwaters, among others.

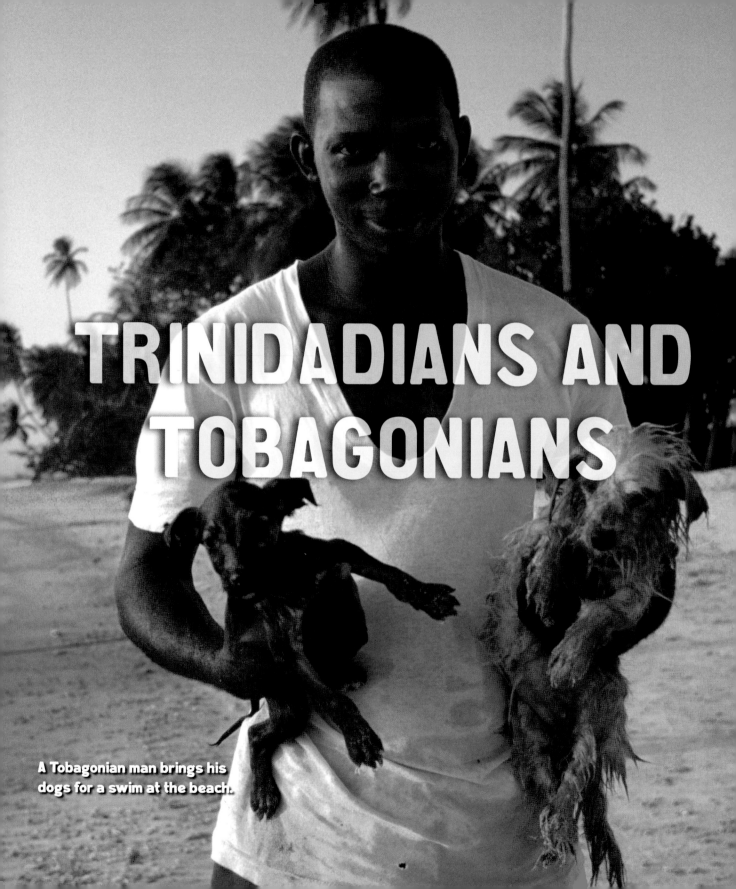

TRINIDADIANS AND TOBAGONIANS

A Tobagonian man brings his dogs for a swim at the beach.

T

RINIDAD AND TOBAGO IS A truly multiethnic country. As of 2005 most (96 percent) of the country's 1.3 million inhabitants resided on the island of Trinidad, with the remainder (4 percent) in Tobago.

The ethnic composition of Trinidad and Tobago reflects a history of conquest and immigration. Two major ethnic groups, Indo-Trinidadian and Tobagonians and Afro-Trinidadian and Tobagonians, account for almost 80 percent of the population, while people of mixed race, European, Chinese, and Syrian-Lebanese descent make up most of the rest of the population.

Schoolgirls smiling for the camera.

Trinidad and Tobago has a fairly average birthrate for the Caribbean, but the high emigration rate keeps the population growth rate fairly low (0.37 percent).

Separated from
Trinidad until
1889, Tobago
has a less rich
ethnic diversity.
Its population of
50,000 is largely
of African descent.

AMERINDIANS

The very first inhabitants of the islands were Amerindians who migrated to the islands from Venezuela. Other Indian groups were the Carib and Arawak. Tobago was uninhabited when Christopher Columbus arrived. In the years of colonial exploitation, few of these people survived as a distinct culture, and almost all had been assimilated into other groups by the end of the 19th century.

EUROPEANS

In Tobago, most
Europeans are
retirees from
Germany and
Scandinavia who
have recently
arrived there.

The next people to arrive on the islands were Europeans—first the Spanish, then the French, and later the English, as well as small numbers of Italians and Portuguese. In the 18th and 19th centuries these people formed the wealthy, ruling aristocratic classes of Trinidad. The French arrived mainly during the Spanish period to take advantage of free agricultural lands. The Portuguese were brought to replace freed African slaves when they refused to accept low wages. The Europeans who remained in Trinidad live in areas in and around Port-of-Spain. About half are of British origin, and the remainder are of French, Italian, Spanish, Portuguese, and German heritage.

AFRICANS

Afro-Trinidadian and Tobagonian make up the country's second-largest ethnic group (about 37.5 percent). The majority are descendants of the colonial slave laborers who were brought in the last few years of Trinidad's Spanish colonial era, and the beginning of the English colonial period. The experience of slavery in Trinidad was limited in that the island was very sparsely populated. The Cedula of Population transformed a small colony of 1,000 in 1773 to a colony with a population of 18,627 by 1797.

MULATTOS

Mulatto is a term used in Trinidad and Tobago to describe people of mixed race. Although they may be of mixed descent, they are culturally part of the black community. But much like the black people in segregated South Africa, there is a small group that considers itself racially distinct and that cultivates marriages with similarly colored mulatto families.

The Cedula of Population was a 1783 edict by the king of Spain related to Trinidad and Tobago. The edict invited anyone of the Roman Catholic faith who would swear loyalty to the Spanish Crown to "take lands of up to 3,000 acres (1,214 ha) free of charge."

Mulattos are of mixed Indian and African ancestry.

INDIANS

Indians make up over 40 percent of the population, the largest ethnic group on Trinidad. Many of them claim a 150-year lineage on the island. They are primarily descendants of indentured workers from India, who were brought to replace freed African slaves who refused to continue working on the sugar plantations. Most of them are farmers who live in the rural areas; the rest are white-collar workers. Indians have moved into small businesses more extensively than people of African descent. Many people of Indian descent have retained their religion and culture, although it has been altered by European and African influences. They are Hindu, Muslim, and Christian by religion. Indian people tend to live as extended families, with several generations of one family living together.

An East Indian wedding. Both bride and groom are in elaborate traditional costumes and headwear.

CHINESE AND LEBANESE

Scattered throughout the world as traders, the Chinese and Lebanese have a strong presence in the chief towns of Trinidad and Tobago, and the Chinese often run the small shops in the villages. Chinese genes have entered into the ethnic mix of Trinidad, and there are many people who have Chinese blood as well as African and Indian.

INTERETHNIC RELATIONS

As diverse as Trinidad and Tobago's population is, the various ethnic groups do not mix freely. At the top of the social hierarchy are the white, descendants of the early settlers, American businessmen, Chinese businessmen, and the Lebanese. Below them on the social scale are educated middle-class blacks and ethnic Indians and businesspeople, and both groups tend to remain apart. There is also little contact between these people and the higher classes.

THE NATIONAL CHARACTER

If Trinidadians and Tobagonians tend to live in well-defined ethnic groups, they share a distinct national character. It was in Trinidad that the festival known as Carnival developed and then spread to the rest of the Caribbean. Carnival is a massive celebration, and it shows how most Trinidadians have a carefree and fun-loving nature. On national festival days everyone celebrates, regardless of the ethnic origin of the festival. All the people of the islands share a taste for food and good eating, and the various cuisines are enjoyed by everyone. All islanders enjoy the national music of calypso. This music also reflects the national character in its refusal to be impressed with anyone or take anything too seriously. At various times of difficulty the islanders have responded by turning the situation into a party or fete. In the 1970s there were curfew fetes, and in the 2009 recession there were recession fetes.

The sense of community among the various ethnic groups is not strong, although there is a vibrant diversity in Trinidadian society.

LIFESTYLE

Young girls waiting to cross the road after visiting the postal agency in Tobago.

FOR THE PEOPLE OF TRINIDAD and Tobago, there are common elements of lifestyle—the climate, economic and physical conditions, life expectancy, education, and health care—but for each of the ethnic groups that live on the islands, there are cultural differences, as well as political divisions, that keep them apart.

Education is an important part of growing up in Trinidad and Tobago. Renowned for its classic German Renaissance architectural structure, Queens Royal College in Port-of-Spain is the oldest secondary school in Trinidad and Tobago.

In Trinidad and Tobago there are few of the uglier aspects of racism. The various cultural groups have intermarried, and at times such as Carnival, they enjoy a common activity. There is also none of the avoidance of racial matters in Trinidad and Tobago that gets labeled as discrimination in Western countries. Trinidadians in particular will discuss skin tone and racial characteristics in a way that many societies do not.

BLACK LIFESTYLE

Afro-Trinidians make up the second-largest ethnic group in Trinidad and Tobago. They are united by their ethnicity and common heritage. Their ancestors arrived on the islands as slaves, either directly in slave ships that had bought them from the west coast of Africa, often Ghana, or as slaves of settlers from other Caribbean islands. If all black people in Trinidad and Tobago have a common outlook on life, it is a laidback one. Characteristic is Carnival, which evolved among the black people of Trinidad as an irreverent and often outrageous celebration.

The diversity of languages and religions that the slaves brought with them to the islands meant that a common tongue and way of life had to evolve. It was black slaves who created the use of pidgin, which has influenced Trinidad English, because they had no common language to share.

Many aspects of African life have remained, but in a highly evolved way. African religions have influenced Trinidad's religions, and the rhythms of

A relaxed lifestyle characterizes the culture of the black people of Trinidad and Tobago.

African music can be heard in the counterpoint rhythms of Carnival. Afro-Trinidans left the countryside after emancipation. This group is chiefly urban and has received a good education. Their religions are often new forms of Christianity, and there are large numbers of Rastafarians. During the 1970s and the upsurge in black power movements in the United States, a particular style of dressing emerged with Afro hairstyles, and loose and brightly patterned African shirts. Today, however, men wear casual T-shirts and slacks in their leisure time. For the office, a tie and short-sleeved shirt are more common. Black people tend to work in white-collar jobs, and for many years, they dominated the civil service.

LIFE IN THE CITY

Trinidad and Tobago has only two cities—Port-of-Spain and San Fernando. Both are in Trinidad. Business hours in these two cities are a little longer than in most European cities, from 8:00 A.M. to 6:30 P.M., and stores stay open late in the evening and on the weekend. Port-of-Spain is the administrative center of the islands, and many civil service workers live there. Besides being a center for administration and banking, Port-of-Spain is an industrial base, with many of its citizens working in sawmills, textile mills, citrus canneries, and the Angostura bitters factory. The city has a major port, and part of the University of the West Indies is close by. San Fernando is located in the oil fields, and most of the people work in the oil industry.

Beautifully landscaped suburban housing close to the city area of Trinidad.

CITY HOMES

In the cities most people live in wooden houses. In the suburbs of Port-of-Spain, these homes seem to disappear into the hills behind the city, where houses perch in steeply sloping yards. Houses are small, often one-story buildings with corrugated iron roofs, but they are in shady suburbs lined with fruit trees and have clean running water and a constant supply of electricity. As people have grown wealthier, they have added on more stories to their houses, which take on a strange, impromptu form as they expand upward. Individual suburbs were developed for the various ethnic groups and are still largely racially divided. Huge brick houses, built in many different styles, stand out among the simpler buildings. Most of them are in the center of cities like Port-of-Spain and are still privately owned or have become government offices.

Trinidadians and Tobagonians often shop in sophisticated malls where expensive imported clothes and electrical goods are displayed in Western-style department stores.

MARKETS

Although Trinidad and Tobago has a fair share of supermarkets where people go to buy expensive imports from the United States, it also has flourishing street markets where people can buy fresh local produce. Fruit stalls line the streets of the cities, and at the harbors, every kind of fish is laid out on stalls for sale. Although some of the street markets are highly regulated, covered markets, others are little shantytowns where the vendors have built rickety buildings along the street or inside unused building sites. Many of the stallholders actually live on the premises, and small villages have sprung up within the city, populated by the stallholders. Craft markets also spring up in tourist areas selling Rastafarian T-shirts and locally made basket ware. Cooked food stalls also line the streets, selling ready-made Chinese, Indian, and Trinidadian meals to office workers.

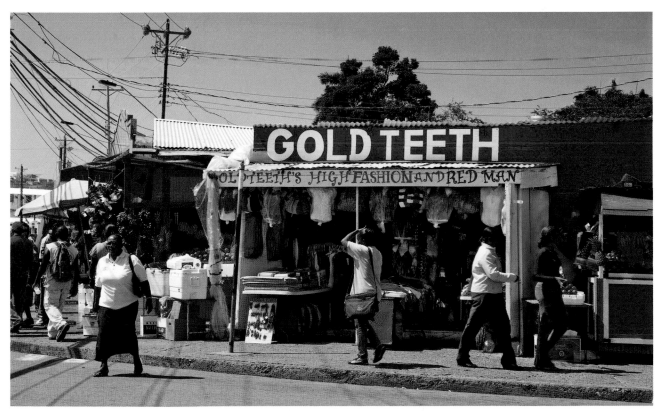

Fashionable clothing being sold at the Carrington Street Scarborough market in Tobago.

INDIAN LIFESTYLE

For a hundred years or more, the Indian population of Trinidad and Tobago consisted of poorly educated field workers, but as education has improved in the last 20 years or so, a demographic change has been taking place, with Indians moving into middle-class, white-collar jobs and into the cities to work.

Because of their origin, many Indian families have retained ties with their ancestral country. Black people arrived in Trinidad and Tobago, most of them unwillingly, because they had been kidnapped in their native home in Africa and taken away from people who shared their languages and customs. Indian people arrived voluntarily, perhaps with friends, and were able to write to family back home. Many Indian businessmen still have ties with their families in India, and as in many other expatriate communities, customs have been fiercely retained in a way that might have slackened a little in the home country.

Women of Indian origins working as chefs in Trinidad.

LIFE IN THE COUNTRY

A farmhouse sits among the lush vegetation in Tobago.

Twenty-five percent of the population of Trinidad and Tobago that lives in the country is mostly located in the south of Trinidad, where there are still large sugar plantations, or in the west of the island around Arouca. Some live in Tobago, which has virtually no big industries. The rural people in Tobago either farm or work in the tourism industry or in the local government.

Life on the big estates is hard, and most estate workers are poor. Most people live in small, single-story wooden houses with tin roofs and often a large overhanging veranda to keep off the sun. They supplement their income with their own fruit and vegetable gardens. There are amenities of modern life at the estate houses, but many of the sugarcane workers belong to an organization called Sou-Sou Land Limited that buys land to develop on behalf of the poor and landless. The poor literally put all their excess cash into savings with the company until they have enough to buy some of its land.

LIFE IN TOBAGO

Trinidad is busy, noisy, polluted in places, and full of congested roads, whereas Tobago is slow and easygoing, with tiny villages dotted around the countryside, and the majority of people work on their own small farms or in tourism. Buildings are all small scale—pretty, bungalow-style cottages. Some of them are the expensive country homes of wealthy Trinidadians, and others are more modest homes of the local people. Roads are narrow and largely unpaved, and some disappear in a bad rainy season. This does not mean that Tobago does not have the dynamic energy of Trinidad—Tobago has its own Carnival and many rural festivals that are celebrated with style and pomp. Most of these festivals are Christian in origin. The only town of any size on Tobago is Scarborough, and this resembles a small country town in Europe rather than a thriving capital city.

Children on an excursion to a nearby shopping mall.

A hospital in Trinidad.

EDUCATION AND HEALTH

In Trinidad and Tobago 98.6 percent of the total population is literate. Education is free and compulsory between the ages of 5 and 16. Trinidad and Tobago is considered one of the most educated countries in the world as it has a literacy rate that exceeds 98 percent. This exceptionally high literacy rate is due to education being free, from kindergarten (preschool) to college.

There are about 500 primary schools on the islands and 100 secondary schools. Secondary education is based on the old British system, where an examination taken at the age of 12 draws out the top students to grammar schools, while those who do not pass the test attend a secondary school where the emphasis is on technical subjects.

There are three universities in Trinidad and Tobago: the University of Trinidad and Tobago, the University of the Southern Caribbean, and the University of the West Indies. The universities all offer degree courses in engineering, law, medicine, education, agriculture, liberal arts, natural science, and social sciences. Technical colleges also provide tertiary education in Port-of-Spain, Centeno, and San Fernando. There are several teacher training colleges. Wealthier students who can afford the fees tend to go to college in the United States. Some private schools are run by Christian groups. In Trinidad and Tobago 90 percent of the households own televisions, and the same percentage of the population owns mobile phones.

White vans with red stripes, called maxi-taxis, are one of the major forms of public transportation.

Children generally start preschool at the early age of three years. Although it is not mandatory for children to start school this early, most Trinidadians and Tobagonians start their children's schooling at this stage because children are expected to have basic reading and writing skills when they begin primary school.

The infant mortality rate in Trinidad and Tobago is 13 per thousand live births, a better average than most Caribbean countries. There are 7.5 doctors for every 10,000 people. Life expectancy is around 70 years, which is very high for the region. Major causes of death are cerebrovascular and heart disease, diabetes, and AIDS. The government runs a national health-care program as well as a compulsory retirement pension plan, and there are benefits for maternity leave, sickness, and industrial injury. About 17 percent of the population lives below the poverty line.

TRANSPORTATION

Public transportation is provided by a government-run bus service (known as the Public Transport Service Corporation or PTSC), privately owned mini-buses (locally known as maxi-taxis), as well as privately owned cars. Maxi-taxis and some cars carry passengers along fixed routes for a fare. Ferries operate between Port-of-Spain and Scarborough. Cars can be brought onto the ferries and kept in the cargo areas. Domestic flights between Port-of-Spain's Piarco International airport and Tobago's Crown Point airport have been operated by Caribbean Airlines since October 2007.

WEDDINGS

In the black community of Trinidad and Tobago, Christianity is often the predominant religion, and couples often prefer a traditional-style wedding, with the bride in a white dress and the groom in a black suit.

Hindu weddings within the Indian community are traditional. Marriages are arranged between families, usually with someone of the same caste. The bride and groom meet a few times before the wedding, and then do not meet at all in the days before the wedding.

THE WHITE LIFESTYLE

Some privileged white citizens of Trinidad and Tobago have lives that are very distant from those of the ordinary people. Their children attend private schools run by the religious orders, and they live in large private estates in the countryside. Their leisure activities separate them from ordinary Trinidadians and Tobagonians, as do their jobs, which are in higher management.

The ticket for the 25-minute flight between Port-of-Spain and Crown Point costs $25 (in U.S. dollars) for one way or $50 for a round trip.

The Trinidadian wedding is usually Westernized, with a white bridal gown, flower girls, and a garden reception.

RELIGION

One of the many majestic Catholic cathedrals that are more modern than colonial in style.

MOST PEOPLE IN TRINIDAD AND tobago practice a religion, with each ethnic group practicing its own religion. Among the whites are the traditional European religions of Roman Catholicism (26 percent of the total population) and Anglicanism (7.8 percent of the total population).

Many black Trinidadians are also Christians, but they practice more recent forms of Christianity, which include Seventh-Day Adventism, Methodism, and Pentecostalism. Other blacks are Rastafarians.

The Hindu Temple in the Sea at Waterloo in Trinidad.

One aspect of Obeah with which many visitors to Trinidad and Tobago are familiar is the Moko-Jumbie, or stilt dancer. In the Trinidad and Tobago Obeah tradition, a Jumbie is an evil or lost spirit. However, the Moko-Jumbie of Trinidad and Tobago is brightly colored, dances in the daylight, and is very much alive.

Among the Indian population are Hindus (22.5 percent of the total population) and Muslims (5.8 percent of the total population), and the small Chinese community practices a mixture of Buddhism and Taoism. A small black Muslim community exists but is entirely separate from the Asian Muslim community.

ORISHA

The slaves who came to Trinidad brought with them elements of their original African religious beliefs. In Trinidad these beliefs became mixed with a Christian faith. Most people of African descent practice the Shango or Orisha, a religion largely found in Tobago. In this form of worship, participants believe that besides an all-powerful God, there are spirits that exist in everything around them. This belief is known as animism. In order to pacify and even to get help from these spirits, one must worship them through ritual dances, offerings, chanting, singing, and prayer.

A woman prepares the iconic offerings for worship.

Orisha originated among the Yoruba, African people who once inhabited an area from Benin to the Niger River but who now live largely in Nigeria. During British rule in Trinidad and Tobago, the religion was suppressed and thus its practice became secretive, and it remains so today. The most notable animist god is Shango, the god of thunder, fire, war, and drumming, who is depicted carrying an ax. Shango is also associated with a Christian saint— Saint Barbara. Another deity of the Orisha religion is Ogun, who is the god of blacksmiths.

Orisha worship takes place in a palais, which is often a sheltered courtyard partly covered by a galvanized roof and decorated with ritual objects such as weapons, jugs, and the materials used during worship, such as wine or oil.

SPIRITUAL BAPTISM

Another form of worship banned by the British, Spiritual Baptism, is a form of Christianity that came to the islands in the 19th century. The religion was officially banned in 1917. The ban was lifted on March 30, 1951, which the Spiritual Baptists celebrate as Shouter Baptist Liberation Day.

The name "Shouter" of the Shouter Baptist faith comes from practitioners' tendency to stand in public places proclaiming their faith.

Devotees dance and enter into a trance at an Orisha Baptist service in Trinidad.

The basis of the faith is the worship of the Holy Trinity—Father, Son, and Holy Spirit—but like Orisha, this faith recognizes animist spirits that must be placated. Outwardly the Shouter Baptist Church looks like any other Christian church, with an altar and rows of pews. But these churches include a center pole from which symbolic objects that are used to call up the animist spirits are hung. Members of the church dress up on Sundays in long white robes and colorful headgear, and attend services that can last up to six hours. The service begins by casting out any unpleasant spirits known as *jumbies* (JUM-bees) that might be in the church. Lighted candles are placed at strategic places, incense is burned, and brass bells are rung. The service proceeds with readings from the Bible to the rhythmic clapping of hands. Like followers of Orisha, members of the congregation become possessed by spirits and shout out loud, often speaking in tongues—that is, in another, unfamiliar language.

RASTAFARIANISM

Rastafarianism, which originated in Jamaica, has become very popular in Trinidad in recent years. It is a Christian-based religion that follows certain texts of the Bible. Rastafarians believe that the late emperor of Ethiopia, Haile Selassie, is the god. Their name for God is Jah. They believe that the emperor was the 225th incarnation of King Solomon, which makes him a modern messiah. Rastafarians do not eat processed food, salt, meat, or dairy products, and do not use any stimulants, although marijuana is used during prayer meetings or meditation. Some of those who practice the religion believe that all black people should return to Ethiopia. Rastafarians typically wear long dreadlocks in keeping with the Bible's exhortation, "They shall not make baldness upon their head, neither shall they shave off the corner of their beard."

According to many Rastafarians, the illegality of marijuana in many nations is evidence that persecution of Rastafarianism is a reality.

Rastafarians, or Rastas, bathing at a rain forest in Trinidad. Rastafarianism is not a highly organized religion but rather an ideology or a way of life.

HINDUISM

Hinduism was introduced in Trinidad and Tobago by the Indian indentured workers, but after 150 years, it has changed quite a lot from the religion that is practiced in India.

Hinduism is polytheistic—Hindus worship a pantheon of gods. At the head of the pantheon is Shiva, the god of creation and destruction. He is depicted with a snake around his neck and a third eye on his forehead and riding a bull. Next in importance is Vishnu, multi-armed and blue, who is said to be the angel of deliverance. Believers think that he will appear on Earth one day and punish the wicked and deliver the pure to heaven. Ganesh, the elephant-headed god, is the god of education and literature. Lakshmi is the goddess of light and prosperity who is worshiped at the Diwali festival. Other gods are Durga, wife of Shiva, depicted wearing a necklace of skulls with blood dripping from her mouth; Saraswati, the goddess of purification; and Hanuman, the demon fighter who invented Sanskrit.

A Hindu temple in Trinidad.

Unlike Hinduism in India, the version in Trinidad and Tobago has almost no vestige of the caste system. In India people marry and accept employment within their caste, but in the islands the only sign of the caste system is the Brahmins of the priestly caste or pundits.

A Hindu religious service in the islands is also different from services in India. The service takes place in the temple as it would in India, but the service, called a *puja* (PU-ja), combines the worship of several deities at once; in India the *puja* is dedicated to only one deity. During the service, the priest arranges votive offerings such as flowers, food, oil, herbs, and pictures of the deity. Then the pundit, a teacher skilled in Hinduism, blesses the arrangements and anoints a flagpole. The deities' flags are hoisted, symbolizing the blessing of the building and the participants.

Hindus in Trinidad and Tobago celebrate Diwali, the Festival of Lights, and Phagwa, the spring festival.

Hindu women encircle a temple of Lord Hanuman in Trinidad. The Hindu deity symbolizes the qualities of an ideal devotee of God.

The Jinnah Memorial Mosque in Saint Joseph in Trinidad is one of the places of worship for Muslims in the city.

ISLAM

Islamic religion originated in seventh-century Arabia through the Prophet Muhammad. Its followers are known as Muslims, and the religion is comprehensive, covering almost every aspect of their lives. It is based on the five pillars of wisdom: the creed, performance of prayer, giving of alms, observance of fasting, and a pilgrimage to Mecca.

The creed can be summed up by the words: there is no God but God, and Muhammad is the prophet of God. There are 28 other prophets, including Jesus Christ, but Muhammad is the most important.

Muslims must pray at least five times a day: at sunrise, noon, late afternoon, sunset, and before bed. A distinctive architectural feature of mosques all over the world as well as in Trinidad and Tobago is the minaret. This is where the muezzin—a chosen Muslim who leads the call to daily prayers from the mosque's minarets—calls the worshipers to prayer.

Part of the African religious traditions in Trinidad and especially in Tobago is a system of natural medicine. Herbal medicines are dispensed by the obeah, but many people know the use of natural herbal remedies. Typical of this kind of medicine is the bush bath. The obeah selects particular herbs and other remedies, and boils them. The infusion is drunk. The herbs must be collected at a certain time depending on the ailment. The cures can be for physical illnesses or psychic ones. Some herbs are cooling, while others are purging. Purging herbs are senna, pawpaw bark, or castor oil. Everyone knows that the use of lemon grass, black sage, and Christmas bush is the remedy for cold. Fevers are treated with lime and Saint John's wort, while Tia Marie leaves cure insomnia.

Muslims are expected to give 2.5 percent of their annual salary to the poor. During the holy month of Ramadan, no food, drink, or tobacco may be consumed between sunrise and sunset. Children begin to take part in the annual fast at about the age of nine. The fifth pillar of the faith is the pilgrimage to Mecca that all Muslims are expected to complete it at least once in their life. There is an unwritten sixth pillar of the faith, the jihad or holy war against the unfaithful.

Most Muslims in Trinidad and Tobago are Shiite. This sect traces its origins back to the time when Ali, the son-in-law and nephew of the Prophet Muhammad, was murdered. Followers of the religion were called Shi'i, meaning "followers of Ali," and this has come to be Shiite.

TRADITIONAL BELIEFS

The hummingbird, which the Caribs believed to be protected by the gods and which was hunted by the Chiman tribe.

Many people in Trinidad and Tobago believe in black magic. *Jumbies* (JUM-bees), or *dih* (DEE) to the Indians, come in many forms. *Douens* (DOO-ens) are the spirits of unbaptized children and are malevolent. Their faces have no features and their feet point backward, so they are easily recognized. People who believe in these spirits seldom speak their children's names aloud for fear that the *douens* might learn them and harm the children.

The *lugarhoo* (LOO-gar-who) feeds on fresh blood and drags iron chains behind it so it can be heard coming. It can change its shape, so superstitious people often hang over the bed a pair of open scissors in the shape of the crucifix to ward off the *lugarhoo*.

A *soucouyant* (SUE-koo-ant) is a female vampire that takes the form of an old woman and lives among the people. She travels around as a ball of fire, keeping her skin in a container while she flies. If the skin is found, covering it with salt is supposed to prevent her from getting back into it.

Among the Carib population, there is a story that explains the origin of the Pitch Lake. The story goes like this: Once the Chiman tribe lived on the site of the lake. At that time the lake did not exist, and the surrounding countryside was fertile and beautiful. The Chiman had a wonderful life, but they became too vain. They began to hunt hummingbirds, which were protected by the gods. In retribution, the gods created the Pitch Lake and buried all the Chiman tribe beneath it.

Another legend tells of the origin of Mount Naparima, which is thought to be the body of Haburi, an Indian hero: In Tobago there is a particularly ferocious story about Mamoo Brebna, who was an African slave. He was so powerful that he was able to stop the sugar mills from working, and when his master tried to beat him, the master's wife felt the pain.

CATHOLICISM AND ANGLICANISM

There are many forms of Christianity in Trinidad and Tobago. Christianity is the official religion, and the predominant form is Roman Catholicism. The tenets of Roman Catholicism are the belief in the Holy Trinity; the veneration of Mary, the mother of Jesus; and the belief in transubstantiation: During the Catholic Mass, the priest performs a ritual in which the communion wafer and wine, through a miracle, "become" the body and blood of Christ. The Anglican Church is very close in ideology and ritual to Roman Catholicism. Both have ornately decorated churches, and in both the priesthood determines church policy, although Anglicans do not recognize the Pope. In addition Holy Communion is treated as simply a symbol of the body and blood of Christ. In both churches worship takes place on Sundays, and in Trinidad and Tobago both religions are practiced chiefly by the white minority. Another Christian denomination, the Presbyterian Church, originated in Scotland and is governed by a body of laymen.

The design of the Church of the Sacred Heart marries Catholic and Anglican traditions.

LANGUAGE

Girlfriends chatting by the
beautiful ocean view in Tobago.

TRINIDAD AND TOBAGO'S official language is English, but many visitors to the country might have considerable trouble recognizing the language spoken on the streets. In official circles, Standard English is the norm, and the more highly educated a person, the closer the dialect will be to Standard English.

A bold advertisement in English flanks a signboard in a protected area in Trinidad and Tobago.

Due to Trinidad's location on the coast of South America, the country has been slowly redeveloping a connection with the Spanish-speaking peoples. In 2004 the government initiated the "Spanish as a Foreign Language (SAFFL) Initiative." People from Venezuela travel to Trinidad and Tobago to learn English, and many English schools have expanded to feature both English and Spanish.

A guide at the Asa Wright Nature Center. Because English is the national language, most tourists have no problem understanding and communicating with the locals.

In Trinidad and Tobago, a Spanish-based creole, known as Coco Payol, was also once widely used. Remnants of Coco Payol still stay in everyday speech.

But in casual conversation and in most informal situations, everybody, including the white elite, uses Trini, a form of English that is based a little on the many languages that have been fed into the culture.

THE FIRST CREOLE

When African slaves were first brought to Trinidad and Tobago, they spoke a multitude of African languages, depending on their place of origin in Africa. In order to communicate with one another and to take orders from their masters, they had to find a lingua franca, a common language that they could all understand. From this need emerged a creole language, based loosely on English but incorporating many African words and expressions. The grammar at first was probably African with English nouns added as a common core of understanding. Each African spoke his or her own language fluently and perhaps a little bit of the other slaves' languages as well, but all their orders came in French, Spanish, or English. Therefore, over generations, the African languages gave way to the languages of the slave masters, and the mother tongue of the slaves became a hybridized language or creole.

For about a hundred years, the language spoken in Trinidad and Tobago was a creole form of French, which was basically French with Twi or Yoruba words included. Even today there is a strong element of French in Trini, and in some rural areas, people still speak a language that is closer to French than to English.

TRINI

The language spoken in Trinidad and Tobago is a mixture of influences from other languages, and it is still changing. In Tobago there have been fewer influences, so the language has fewer Hindi additions and is a closer mix of African and English languages. But Trini is not just a collection of borrowed nouns and a few odd phrases. It has a special quality of its own that reflects the national character. Trini, for example, uses many more double entendres than British or American English. One explanation for this manner of saying one thing but meaning another is that during slavery, the slaves had to be careful of what they said in front of their masters and so developed this way of speaking.

Patois (a variety of Spanish/French) was once the most widely spoken language in Trinidad, and there are various remnants of the language in everyday speech.

Most locals, such as this fruit store vendor, speak to each other in Trini.

Many of the expressions peculiar to Trinidad and Tobago are connected with having fun, relaxing, enjoying Carnival, and other aspects of social life. In businesses and schools, Standard English is used, so it is only on the streets that the really colorful sayings can be heard. Here are some of them.

bashment	a big party or a festival that went really well
beastly	very cold beer
big up	bragging and praising someone else at the same time
boldfaced	being pushy, promoting yourself
break a lime	leave a party when it is at its height
darkers	sunglasses
dou dou	sweetheart
ignorant	quick to take offense
jammin	working hard
liming	having a good time with your friends
sweetman	a man who is supported by his girlfriend
Tobago love	not showing your real feelings

THE FRENCH INFLUENCE

There are many French expressions and words in Trini. Most of the words that describe the jumbies of superstition are of French derivation. Also, many words for plants are French in origin. If someone spreads spiteful gossip about a neighbor, it is called *mauvais langue* (bad language). The French influence is even more noticeable in Trini syntax. In French, describing the weather involves the verb *faire*, "to do" or "to make," so that a French person would say *Il fait brillait*—"the weather is fine." In Trini, French words are directly translated into English, but the structure remains French so that a Trinidadian might say "It making hot" instead of "It is hot."

HINDI

The Indian workers who came to Trinidad and Tobago were different from the African slaves, as they came with a common culture and language and maintained their own language as indentured workers. Hindi, the language that most of them spoke, is still used in the Indian community, although it is rarely spoken in the workplace or at mixed social events. Younger people tend to be more fluent in Trini or Standard English.

Most of the indentured workers lived in specific rural areas of Trinidad and still make up a large portion of the community in the south and east of the island. It is possible to see the continuing development of Trini as a language in the way that Hindi has influenced the creole that is being spoken in Trinidad. Indian workers are still largely associated with small holdings as vegetable growers, so many of the words for vegetables have two options—one is the older English, French, or Spanish word, and the other is a newer, Hindi one. In Trinidad and Tobago the bulbous, purple vegetable that Americans call an eggplant is known as *melongene*, from an early French word. Now it is also called *beigun*, from Hindi. English speakers call it *aubergine*.

SPANISH

The original language of the first European settlers in Trinidad, Spanish, has left fewer marks on Trini English than the other languages, despite the fact that Spanish is the dominant language of South America. It can be found

Indian boys playing in the sand at the Maracas Bay beach in Trinidad. Even though most members of the younger generation converse mainly in English, many still understand Hindi.

Schoolchildren learning English in a classroom. Because the main language used by the media in Trinidad and Tobago is English, children are much more inclined to excel in the language.

as names of many places on the islands—San Rafael, Las Cuevas, Sangre Grande, Los Iros, and many more. Trinidad itself has Spanish origins. Words for types of food and drink have also retained a Spanish flavor such as *pelau*, *sancoche*, *pastelle*, *sapodilla*, and *granadilla*, all types of fruit.

THE MEDIA

Trinidad has two daily broadsheet newspapers, the conservative *Trinidad Guardian* and the more liberal *Independent*. More popular and widely read are the tabloid daily newspapers, which are photograph-oriented and full of local gossip, the *Express* and *Newsday*. Also popular are the evening newspapers, the *Sun* and the *Evening News*. All of these papers have large weekend versions full of color supplements, arts sections, sports sections, and cartoons, but more popular than any of these on the weekends are the scandal sheets—*Bomb*, *Blast*, *Heat*, and *Sunday Punch*, which are full of gossip, pictures of scantily clad women, and huge, shocking headlines. In Tobago the single paper is *Tobago News*, published on Fridays, so most Tobagonians read the Trinidad papers. Trinidadians and Tobagonians are also fond of foreign magazines, which are readily available in the cities. Trinidad produces two glossy magazines of its own: *Ibis*, which focuses on local cultural events, and *Esse*, a women's magazine.

Television is not as ubiquitous in Trinidad and Tobago as in the United States; only about one-eighth of the population owns a television. There are three terrestrial TV channels, the state-owned TTT station, and two commercial channels. Popular programs include American soaps such as *The Bold and the Beautiful*, situation comedies, American game shows, and lots of music programs that focus on local music and musicians, particularly late at night when there are live broadcasts. Most set owners also have access to cable TV where many American channels such as CNN, Discovery, and HBO broadcast directly into the home. American television programs are also available via satellite.

Radio is more popular than television. The best radio caters to local taste with talk shows and news about big parties and upcoming fetes. Music stations broadcast almost nonstop calypso between November and February before the annual calypso competition, after which the airwaves resound to the music of reggae. There are about 14 Trinidad-based radio stations, one dedicated entirely to Indian movie music and Indian reggae, three to popular music and talk, and several to classical and middle-of-the-road music.

Trinidadians having a ball at a concert. With better access to information through the country's developing media, more and more young people become familiar with Western pop culture.

ARTS

A brightly colored art mural adorns a wall outside
Queens Park Cricket Club in Port-of-Spain in Trinidad.

THE RICH CULTURE OF Trinidad and Tobago manifests itself in a variety of artistic forms, but music is unquestionably the most vibrant and influential way that people of the two islands express themselves.

A painter at work in Pigeon Point in Tobago. The idyllic natural environment found in Trinidad and Tobago is a source of inspiration to many artists.

STEEL SOUNDS

The steel band is one of the country's most distinctive contributions to world music, and it reflects the talent of ordinary people who may not be able to read a musical score but who are nonetheless able to play an astonishing variety of different types of music. This variety extends from internationally recognized classical pieces by composers like Mozart to contemporary music written for and by working-class musicians who seek to comment on social and political life.

The steel drum, more commonly known as the pan, is the defining instrument of the steel band. Its well-documented origin goes back to the 1930s when empty oil drums were first used instead of the bottles, garbage can lids, and other materials that had been used by percussion musicians who were too poor to afford anything else.

The Black Rock Church in Trinidad and Tobago is decorated with brightly colored frescoes of stories from the Bible.

PARANG

The music of Trinidad and Tobago is a synthesis of African and European musical traditions that has its origins in the arrival of Spanish colonizers at the end of the 15th century. The Spanish introduced Christmas carols, and today, the legacy of this can be heard in traditional Christmas music known as *parang* (par-ANG). This kind of music is heard throughout the month of December and into January, and the musicians are known as *parranderos* (par-an-DARE-owes).

THE MIGHTY SPARROW

One of the figures most closely associated with the rich talent produced by the craze for calypso is a musician who was never called simply by his surname, which is Sparrow, but always by the epithet of Mighty Sparrow. He first emerged in the 1950s, and his musical abilities coincided with the growing popularity of the long-playing record (LP). This allowed musicians with the necessary talent to develop a repertoire of pieces that could make up the extended number of tracks that the LP allowed. Until the advent of the LP, a band would release just two tracks, one on each side of the short-playing record. Sparrow produced his first LP in 1957, and with his own recording company, he went on to regularly release an album each year. When the new government established by Eric Williams in 1956 introduced the Calypso King musical competition, the Mighty Sparrow won.

CALYPSO MEETS DISCO POP

By the late 1970s it seemed to some musicians that calypso was losing its verve, especially in the face of competition from the growing globalization of pop and disco music. Rather than having a slow death, calypso bounced back with a vengeance, and the new sound was christened *soca*.

The musician most closely associated with the birth of soca is Lord Shorty or, as he is now known, Ras Shorty I. He sped up the tempo of calypso and

A calypso singer belts out a tune against the natural backdrop.

Women in costumes dancing at the Mardi Gras Carnival in Trinidad.

made it more compatible with the funky dance music that was sweeping across the United States. The synthesizers and other electronic aids to musical composition that were fuelling the disco craze also found a place in the rejuvenated calypso sound.

Soca is currently the most popular form of calypso music in Trinidad and Tobago, and it dominates the big festivals, especially Carnival. There is now a well-established annual competition that, echoing the Calypso King event, awards the title of the Soca Monarch to the victor. Super Blue, Chinese Laundry, KMC, and Tony Prescott are currently some of the most popular soca musicians. Their new releases are eagerly awaited by the public.

Not to be left behind by the trend, Indians have evolved their own version of soca. It carries the delightful appellation of chutney soca. This is a unique musical form and is evidence of the astonishing richness and creativity of cultural life in Trinidad and Tobago. Chutney soca displays the same fast-paced tempo of traditional soca, but married to and merging with the sound of sitars and Hindi and English lyrics. The synthesis is mirrored in the dance movements of chutney soca, which manage to combine the gusto of calypso dancing with the highly formalized hand and arm movements of classical Indian dance.

LITERATURE

The creative and imaginative use of language as an art form does more than make itself felt in the clever lyrics and verbal puns that form so essential part of the musical tradition of calypso. The country's literary tradition can be traced back to at least the 1930s when a diverse group of young writers began to experiment with different literary forms. Short stories and poems began to appear in print, and soon the novels made their first appearance.

Winner of the 1992 Nobel Prize for Literature, Derek Walcott directs a rehearsal of his play *Odysseus* in Saint Lucia.

Derek Walcott's works are extremely popular among people who are interested in the cultural diversity of his country.

After World War II, Samuel Selvon, a local writer, made an impact with his humorous novel *A Brighter Sun*, and this was followed by the more gritty *The Lonely Londoners*. This novel, set in London in the postwar era, told the sad reality of the racism that immigrants from Trinidad and Tobago often encountered when they came to Britain to start a new life. Equally influential has been the work of Earl Lovelace, especially his powerful novel *The Dragon Can't Dance*, which explores the phenomenon of Carnival.

Alongside the novelist V. S. Naipaul, the local poet Derek Walcott has achieved the most in establishing the international renown of Trinidadian literature. Walcott was born in 1930 on the island of Saint Lucia, but after studying at a university in Jamaica, he moved to Trinidad, where he became a journalist and lived for decades. He published poetry and plays, and in 1957 he went to New York to study about theaters. Two years later he founded and directed the Trinidad Theater Workshop and out of this artistic venture emerged a number of talented actors. In 1992 Walcott was awarded the Nobel Prize for Literature, the most prestigious literary award in the world.

V. S. NAIPAUL

The novelist whose work and influence has made itself most powerfully felt around the world is V. S. Naipaul. He was born in 1932 into a family that had emigrated from India. His father was a noted journalist who also published a collection of short stories. Naipaul did well at school and won a scholarship that took him to Oxford University in England, where he studied literature.

His first novel appeared in the 1950s, but it was the publication of A House for Mr. Biswas *in 1961 that established his fame as a writer. After traveling through the Caribbean, he published* The Middle Passage *in 1961 and expressed the view that the West Indies was a home to displaced people who did not have their own cultural identity. This point of view, and his exposure of the corrupting effect of colonialism in places like Trinidad, did not always endear him to establish figures in his country.*

DEREK WALCOTT

Derek Walcott is another famous writer in Trinidad and Tobago. In 1962 Walcott brought out a collection of his poetry, entitled In a Green Night: Poems 1948—1960, *and like much of his early work, the poems proclaimed with affection about the natural beauty of the West Indies. Walcott's work examines the predicament of coming from a black culture and yet being influenced by a mainstream European culture. Many of his poems in* The Gulf *(1969) express his personal sense of alienation in being caught between two very different cultures. In* Midsummer *(1984), Walcott also explores the experience of being a black writer in the United States and the way this affects his view of his own Caribbean background.*

Walcott has also written a number of plays. Those most often produced on stage are Dream on Monkey Mountain *and* Pantomine. *His most recent poetic work is* Omeros, *hailed by many critics as one of the most significant works of Caribbean literature. The poem takes its inspiration from the ancient Greek epic of Homer's* Odyssey *and uses the tale of a man trying to return home as an extended metaphor for the plight of West Indians who also find themselves cut off from their own cultural and spiritual homeland.*

VISUAL ARTS

The literary and oral tradition are so well developed in Trinidad and Tobago that the visual arts are usually relegated to a role of secondary importance in the arts. This is hardly fair because the roots of the islands' visual culture go back as far as the oral tradition and are very much a part of everyday cultural life. The best expression of the inventive and highly creative imagination of the islands' visual art is found in the rich variety of designs and motifs created for the multitude of Carnival bands. These designs call upon a number of artistic skills, like copper beating and the dexterous use of fiberglass molds, as well as a flair for eye-catching and sometimes outrageous motifs.

Two screaming masks face off with each other in Trinidad. These masks are part of elaborate costumes worn during festive periods in the country.

LEISURE

A group of men playing cards at a social club in Tobago. Hanging out and relaxing is one of the most popular pastimes in Trinidad and Tobago.

THE PEOPLE OF TRINIDAD AND Tobago revel in their leisure time. There is a whole vocabulary of Trini English dedicated solely to the topic of leisure, especially things connected with the great festival of Carnival.

Having a good time with your friends in Trinidad and Tobago is better known locally as "liming," and there is a whole set of rules about how to lime successfully.

Fishing is a popular activity among the local people.

A goat racing competition in Tobago. Competitions such as these are a good source of fun.

Besides hanging out with their friends, the people of the islands also enjoy many other pursuits. Sports, such as soccer, golf, and water activities, are extremely popular, and the beaches and city parks are excellent places for these activities. In addition, technology also affects people's lives, providing entertainment such as soap operas, documentaries, and movies on television, as well as news and music on the radio.

LIMING

Liming is an activity that particularly appeals in Trinidad. It has no particular structure to it. Liming can take place in someone's home, on the beach, on the street, or at a calypso performance. A good limer has lots of time to spend and knows how to appreciate doing nothing. A typical lime might be hanging outside a department store, in the park, or in someone's yard. Leaving a liming session when it is going really well, or "breaking a lime," is a bad social gaffe. When someone does this, it reminds all the other limers that they also have something to do, and that they also ought to leave. This is bad for the party, and so the accusation of breaking a lime is a particularly bad one.

CALYPSO

Calypso is not just a musical form in Trinidad and Tobago, but it is a way of life. Calypso is on the radio every day and is a powerful form of social criticism. In the islands, people spend much of their leisure time discussing the latest calypso song and analyzing the lyrics, which can often be obscure to someone who does not follow the political scene. Calypso is known as the poor people's newspaper, and songs often say in an obscure way things that would lead to libel actions if they were said by a politician.

Every year in Trinidad, there is a calypso competition. Long before the event begins, calypso players set up huge marquee tents to practice. Anyone can join the players in their tents and listen to their music.

Teenage boys relaxing outside a beach shack in Tobago.

Locals enjoying an open-air concert in Trinidad.

OPEN-AIR CONCERTS

When the calypso season is over, young people like to spend the summer listening to reggae and rapso music. This is played widely on the radio, but there are also large open-air concerts where well-known and lesser-known reggae and rapso artists perform. The concert might take place in one of the city's parks with a deejay playing lots of music from Jamaica as well as local bands performing live. Rapso is the Trinidad and Tobago form of reggae and involves African drumbeats and spoken lyrics, often of a political nature. Young people will happily spend the night and early hours dancing to local bands. These big parties or concerts are known locally as fetes.

Nightclubs are also very popular after work and especially on the weekends. They open late, at about 10:00 P.M., and their closing times usually specify "till," which means they are open till the last person has gone home. Nightclubs are usually out of town and more sophisticated and expensive than fetes.

DRUGS

Like many countries Trinidad and Tobago has a drug scene. Although drugs, including marijuana, are illegal, and people are regularly warned against using cannabis, there is a strong counterculture of people who use marijuana in order to lime or hang out with their friends, though it is not done openly.

SHOPPING

Trinidad, in particular, is full of shopping malls that are dedicated to American and European designer clothes. In the 1970s, during the oil boom, there was a general feeling of wealth, and many people flew to the United States for a weekend's shopping. Recently the poorer economic climate has reduced this activity. But Trinidadians love to shop, even if only to look at the goods being offered. Shopping extends also to the little stores and stalls on the streets, and a great deal of liming can take place during a shopping trip when friends meet outside a store or on the street.

A man peddles his accessories on a beach in Tobago. Work and leisure are seldom separate in the minds of Trinidadians and Tobagonians, who approach work with a relaxed attitude.

DWIGHT YORKE

Dwight Yorke is one of the most successful soccer players in Europe. He plays for Manchester United, one of Great Britain's most successful teams, along with numerous other soccer superstars. Born and brought up in Tobago, were he learned to play, Yorke was hired by Manchester for 12.5 million pounds (US$ 19.5 million). When interviewed about his successful adaptation to the limelight, playing for an internationally renowned soccer team, he said: "It is not pressure. Pressure is Kosovo, where people are not getting food and their country is getting bombed. I call this enjoyment. You play soccer, you express yourself in front of a lot of people, and you get paid a fantastic amount of money to do things you always dreamed of doing. That to me is a great time."

SPORTS

The national pastime of Trinidad and Tobago is cricket. Most parks have several cricket pitches, and small cricket matches are played on the streets by children. Cricket is a game that is most common to the British Commonwealth countries, and its rules are very complex. Cricket matches often take days to play.

Trinidad and Tobago ranks 91st out of 195 countries in the world in the world soccer rankings.

Kids playing cricket at Charlotteville in Tobago.

Men enjoying a soccer game.

In Trinidad and Tobago watching cricket as well as playing it is a favorite pastime. Most professional matches take place in March and April in Port-of-Spain. The events include very loud soca music, lots of cold drinks, and cheering on the teams when someone begins a series of runs. Much liming goes on at cricket matches.

Soccer, called football, is another game that local people, whether young or old, enjoy tremendously. When children are not playing cricket in the street, they are invariably playing soccer.

Some more expensive and elite sporting activities involve water sports such as sailing, surfing, and scuba diving around the reefs off Tobago. Less elitist are windsurfing and swimming, although swimming off the shore can be quite dangerous. There are windsurfing competitions in the islands each year.

Golf is also quite an expensive sport, and most people who play golf belong to an exclusive golf club. There are several golf courses in Trinidad and one in Tobago, all privately owned. There are no public golf courses.

Scouting was founded in Trinidad and Tobago in 1911, and Trinidad and Tobago became a member of the World Organization of the Scout Movement in 1963.

SCOUTING

Most children in Trinidad and Tobago attend church, temple, or mosque, and a large part of their weekends is taken up with religious activities. Another activity for young people is scouting. The Scout Movement was introduced from the United Kingdom, where it was once very popular. The Scout Movement in Trinidad and Tobago has a strong following. Scout troops wear a special uniform, and their activities involve hiking in the countryside, camping, and practicing Scouting skills such as flower identification, first aid, survival, swimming, and safety. Scout groups meet once a week in the evenings and study for a series of badges in each skill.

Scouting equips these children with essential skills for survival and teaches them independence.

QUEEN'S PARK SAVANNAH

The Brian Lara Pavilion at Queens Park Savannah's Cricket Club.

Port-of-Spain is a dusty, busy city. Leisure activities are often centered on the Queen's Park Savannah. Some people in Port-of-Spain say that the huge park is like an enormous traffic circle in the middle of the city, and that all traffic weaves its way around it. The park has a circumference of 2.3 miles (3.7 km) and is the largest open space in the city. It was established as a park in 1814 and has served as the city's outdoor living room ever since. The park is useful for many leisure pursuits. During the hot working hours, the park is relatively empty, but after about 4:00 P.M., it comes alive with a myriad of activities. Part of the park is divided into soccer fields, and they are constantly full of players. Other areas are dedicated to cricket. Joggers do circuits of the many paths around the park.

At the southern end of the park is the old racetrack. The races have moved to Arima, but the former grounds are home to all the biggest festivals in town and many smaller fetes. The streets outside the park are lined with vans and trucks selling plenty of good food.

Until the early 1990s horse racing was held frequently at the Queen's Park Savannah racetrack.

FESTIVALS

Carnival participants parade
around in stilts in Trinidad.

TRINIDAD AND TOBAGO IS made for festivals both because of its pleasant climate and the disposition of its people. The really big festival in Trinidad is Carnival on the Monday and Tuesday before Lent begins.

In total there are 13 other official public holidays where all the workplaces close, shops have special sales, and special events and concerts are held to mark the event. Public holidays reflect the islands' cultural diversity with Muslim, Christian, Hindu, Catholic, and Baptist celebrations. A current issue is the lack of a special celebration for the Chinese citizens.

Carnival paraders dressed in their artistic and colorful costumes.

Celebrating a festival is not restricted to any one group or religion; festivals are celebrated by everybody. Indians enjoy Carnival as much as the next person, while Christians happily light a little oil lamp for the Indian festival of light, Diwali.

CARNIVAL

This is really the festival to end all festivals. Trinidadians and Tobagonians sneer at the South American equivalents. Carnival has its origins in Europe in Roman times in the festival of Saturnalia, a midwinter festival celebrating the beginning of the New Year. By the Middle Ages it had become the Feast of Fools, a final celebration before the 40 days of fasting and denial of Lent. The event was always an outrageous affair, frowned on by the Church.

Children get swept up in the infectious Carnival spirit, dressing up and performing.

French planters brought Carnival to Trinidad in the 18th century. Originally the festival was a serious religious affair with great balls where white planters wore fancy clothes and impressed their neighbors. While the planters drank wine and wore masks, the slaves out in the yard had their own party that gradually took over the celebration in the years after emancipation. Over time African elements entered the torchlit Carnival processions, which spilled into the streets with drumming, costumes, and lots of noise. Originally Carnival was three days of celebration before Ash Wednesday, but celebrations on the first day, Sunday, were banned by the British authorities. The more the authorities disapproved of Carnival, the more essential and wild it became, drawing in the descendants of the French planters and the middle-class Mulatto population. In 1881 a group of British soldiers was ordered to calm down the procession but caused a riot instead. The authorities banned some of the more lewd characters in the Carnival procession, African drumming was banned, and finally the torches were outlawed as a fire hazard.

Carnival gives ample opportunities for the locals to get creative with their costumes.

Carnival became a quieter affair but was never really quashed. In the 1890s a series of competitions was encouraged by the government to help clean up the event. First there was a band competition, then a calypso competition, a costume competition, and others. In the 1940s someone discovered the use that could be made of old U.S. army oil drums, and the steel band was invented. In 1956, after a few war years when it was banned, Carnival came back with the Calypso King competition and has never looked back.

Every year, Carnival reflects the political issues of the times. In the black power years of the 1960s, the masqueraders dressed to tell the story of white control over the economy; in the 1970s they focused on women's rights.

HOSAY

When this festival was first celebrated in Trinidad in 1884, it was a sad and solemn affair commemorating the martyrdom of some early Muslim leaders. But after 150 years the event has turned into a joyous and noisy occasion

Some stage performances depict iconic moments of local history or current social issues.

celebrated by all Trinidadians. In the past wailing women walked through the streets crying out behind replicas of the tombs of the martyrs. Nowadays fire-eaters, Indian drummers, and whirling dancers are the order of the day.

The festival begins with Flag Night, when colorful flags are paraded around the town to represent the battle of Kerbela. The next day a procession is held, led by elaborate models of the martyrs' tombs made from bamboo, paper, and tinfoil. The procession includes dancers and drumming. On the third night of the festival, huge models of the tombs are paraded around the town, followed by two huge moons representing the martyrs themselves and carried by special dancers who dance around as if in a trance while carrying the enormously heavy poles with moons at the top. At midnight the two moons are brought into contact to symbolize the two martyr brothers' triumph over death. All this is done to the rhythm of the Indian tassa drums. Dancers perform a stick dance playing out a mock battle with stick and shield. On the final day, the moons and tombs are taken to the sea, where they are cast on the water after prayers.

Muslim women in Trinidad during Hosay. Trinidadians celebrate Hosay with a procession consisting of elaborately decorated tomb and Indian drummers.

The celebrations of Diwali continue for over a week, and the headquarters of the National Council of Indian Culture at Diwali Nagar becomes the focal point of the celebrations.

DIWALI

Between late October and early November, the Indian festival of lights is held to honor the goddess Lakshmi and to celebrate the triumph of good over evil. In the weeks before the event, Diwali Queens are chosen rather in the way of modern beauty pageants, with the competitors wearing Indian dress rather than bathing suits. There are also concerts and musical competitions. On the night before little oil lamps known as *deyas* are lit all over the house to light the goddess's way. All over towns that celebrate the event, the small lamps are supported by strings of colored electric lights. It is this show that has encouraged non-Hindus to enjoy the festival. On Diwali people exchange gifts, and there is feasting in every house.

Indian dancers take a break during Diwali. Indians celebrate Diwali with a brightly lit replica of the goddess Lakshmi, while beautiful fan-shaped lights decorate the front of each Indian house.

EID AL-FITR

The festival of Eid al-Fitr marks the Muslim New Year. Each year, the imams decide the day long in advance. The date varies from year to year because it is determined by the lunar calendar. It is preceded by a month of fasting from dawn till dusk. On the day itself, there is a visit to the mosque, and alms are given to the poor. Everyone wears new clothes, and houses are thoroughly cleaned. There are official dinners during which people from other religions attend, and the traditional dish *sawine* (SAY-wine) is served. This is prepared with vermicelli boiled in milk with raisins, sugar, and chopped almonds. In private homes the family gathers for a similar celebration of the end of Ramadan and a sense of renewal and spiritual cleanliness. Unlike other celebrations, this one has not given way to the usual wild partying, and remains a quiet family affair.

The name Hosay comes from *Husayn* (also spelled Hussein, the grandson of the Prophet Muhammad) who was assassinated by Yazid, a renegade Muslim leader.

A mosque in Trinidad. After visiting the mosque on the morning of Eid al-Fitr, Muslim men return to their homes and join the rest of the family in a sumptuous lunch. Children are given candy and money.

FOOD

A woman selling her homemade pepper sauces.

THE FOOD OF TRINIDAD AND Tobago reflects the diversified culture of the islands, so no single dish represents the national cuisine. This is not due to any inadequacy in the food, but to many different cultures that have influenced the kind of food that is eaten.

The result is a mouth-watering blend of tastes and styles that include African, Indian, South American, European, Chinese, and Caribbean.

Trinidad and Tobago has a rich variety of animal life. However, Trinidadians and Tobagonians no longer hunt and eat wild animals because many are endangered.

Food shacks like these are found all over the beaches of Trinidad and Tobago. Many also whip up quick treats.

Creole food served in a restaurant in Trinidad.

The people of Trinidad and Tobago love food because it is a part of enjoying life and socializing with others. Any excuse is a reason for preparing something tasty to eat, and offering food to a guest is very much a part of the island's etiquette.

CREOLE FOOD

The term *creole*, when applied to food in Trinidad and Tobago, refers to those dishes and styles of cooking that have their origins in Africa. Along the way European culture has also made itself felt, so that creole cooking is an amalgam of different influences working on an African cuisine.

Pelau (PEL-ow) is a typical and highly popular creole dish that uses chicken, savory pigeon peas, and other vegetables along with garlic, peppers, and onions. The ingredients are cooked in coconut milk and served with rice. What gives *pelau* its appealing taste is the mixture of spices that are added. Although the exact balance of spices is up to the cook, cinnamon is usually part of the mixture.

NATIONAL FOOD SECURITY PROGRAM

Fresh, local produce sold at a market in Trinidad.

Trinidad and Tobago is now trying to launch a National Food Security Program in which 25 percent of all food consumed is domestically produced. Despite domestic food production, Trinidad and Tobago still remains a net importer of food, with the conversion of its economy from an agricultural base to an industrialized base. The National Food Crop Farmers Association (NFFA) in Trinidad and Tobago claims that the government favors megafarms rather than the small-time farmer struggling to make a living. To make things worse, Trinidad and Tobago faced a water shortage and extremely dry weather in March 2010, threatening to drive up food prices. Trinidad and Tobago's farmers were also up in arms due to attempts by the Water and Sewage Authority (WASA) to have them obtain water licenses that the farmers would have to pay for, adding to their woes.

On the bright side, May 14, 2010, was the official end of the dry season as Trinidad and Tobago experienced six hours of nonstop rain, giving relief to the farmers. In March 2009 the National Food Crop Farmers Association confirmed that a recently formed partnership with the Guan Dong Chinese Agriculture Institute of Technology and Machinery would give the local sector a much-needed boost. Under the plan that would last for three years, local farmers would be exposed to training and technology in several areas, such as organic farming, processing, and fish farming.

CALLALOO (CARIBBEAN VEGETABLE SOUP)

4 servings

12 sweet potato leaves or bunch of spinach

¼ pound (110 g) salted beef or ham bone (optional)

¼ pound (110 g) salted pork

2 cups (500 ml) coconut milk

1 tablespoon (15 ml) butter

1 medium green pepper

8 okras

2 sprigs of thyme

1 medium onion

4 chives

Boiling water (enough to cover)

- Clean the sweet potato leaves.
- Wash and cut up the okra, then soak and cut the meat.
- Put all the ingredients into a pot with enough boiling water to cover and simmer until soft.
- Blend everything with a mixer until slightly creamy.
- Serve over rice.

COCONUT SUGAR CAKE

8 servings

2 cups (500 ml) granulated sugar

1 teaspoon (5 ml) rum

½ cup (125 ml) water

1 cup (250 ml) grated coconut

⅓ cup (85 ml) raisins

- Boil sugar and water together until syrupy.
- Test a few drops in a saucer with cold water.
- When it forms a soft ball, remove from the heat.
- Cool a little, and then beat the mixture until it gets very thick and begins to crystallize.
- Stir in rum and coconut.
- Work quickly and do not overbeat the mixture.
- Blend well and pour into a greased shallow pan (8 inches × 8 inches x 1 inch).
- Cut into 2-inch squares when hardened.

Note: It is traditional in Trinidad and Tobago to dye the mixture half pink.

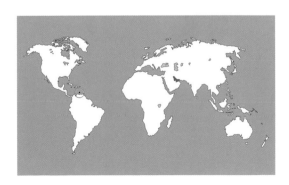

ECONOMIC TRINIDAD AND TOBAGO

Natural Resources

 Asphalt

 Natural gas

Petroleum

Agriculture

 Citrus

 Cocoa

 Coffee

 Rice

 Vegetables

Services

 Airport

 Port

 Tourism

ABOUT THE ECONOMY

OVERVIEW

The twin-island nation of Trinidad and Tobago experienced 16 consecutive years of real GDP growth through 2008. Long-term growth prospects nevertheless remain promising, as Trinidad and Tobago further develops its oil and gas resources and the industries dependent on natural gas, including petrochemicals, fertilizers, iron/steel, and aluminum. Additional growth potential also exists in financial services, telecommunications, and transportation. Trinidad and Tobago has made a transition from an oil-based economy to one based on natural gas. Natural gas production continues to expand and should meet the needs of new industrial plants coming on stream over the next few years. The petrochemical sector includes plants that produce methanol, ammonia, urea, and natural-gas liquids. The government is also seeking to diversify the economy to reduce dependence on the energy sector and to achieve self-sustaining growth.

GROSS DOMESTIC PRODUCT (GDP)

$25.21 billion (2008 estimate)

CURRENCY

ETrinidad and Tobago dollar (TT$)
1 US$ = TT $6.25 (2010 estimate)

LABOR FORCE

629,000 (2009 estimate)

LABOR FORCE BY TYPE OF JOB

agriculture: 5.3 percent
industry: 34 percent
services: 60.7 percent (2005 estimate)

UNEMPLOYMENT RATE

5.1 percent (2008 est.)

NATURAL RESOURCES

Petroleum, natural gas, and asphalt

AGRICULTURE

Cocoa, rice, citrus, coffee, vegetables, poultry

MAIN INDUSTRIES

Engineering, electronics, wood and wood products, textiles, information technology, telecommunications

MAIN EXPORTS

Petroleum and petroleum products, liquified natural gas, methanol, ammonia, urea, steel products, beverages, cereal and cereal products, cocoa, coffee, citrus fruit, vegetables, and flowers

MAIN IMPORTS

Mineral fuels, lubricants, machinery, transportation equipment, manufactured goods, food, chemicals, and live animals

CULTURAL TRINIDAD AND TOBAGO

Little Tobago Island
Little Tobago Island on the extreme east end of Tobago across from Speyside is an uninhabited bird sanctuary with several miles of trails. Its most spectacular views are from the hills overlooking the seaward direction. Regularly scheduled glass-bottomed boats ferry visitors to the island, revealing the coral reefs below.

Mount Saint Benedict Monastery
The church tower sitting on the Northern Range Hills above Tunapuna is one of the most striking landmarks east of Port-of-Spain. This Benedictine Monastic community is the largest and oldest in the Caribbean. It was established in 1912 by monks fleeing Brazil's attempt to take over their land.

Buccoo Reef and Speyside
Tobago's fringing coral reefs are some of the best in the region, and because of its nutrient-rich coastal waters, they are also home to an impressive abundance of marine life, ranging from the microscopic to the huge. Large marine animals frequently seen are sea turtles, reef sharks, hammerhead sharks, groupers, eagle rays, and manta rays.

National Museum and Art Gallery, Port-of-Spain
The local flavor of the museum is conveyed by an extensive display on the evolution of the pans, masks, and costumes used during Carnival. Industrial histories include sugar, cocoa, and coconut agriculture. A small display features Angostura Bitters, which were invented here in the late 19th century.

Asa Wright Nature Center and Lodge
This is located in an unspoiled rain forest covered range of mountains that runs from west to east across the top of Trinidad. The bird species found at the site and which come to the feeders off the veranda are some of the most colorful in Trinidad.

Caroni Sanctuary
This sanctuary is a series of mangrove-lined waterways and lakes, the nesting location of the stunning scarlet ibis, national bird of Trinidad and Tobago. There are also little herons, egrets, and cormorants. Viewing of the birds is done when one cruises up and down the waterways.

Nariva Swamp
The Nariva Swamp is the largest freshwater wetland in Trinidad and Tobago and has been designated a Wetland of International Importance under the Ramsar Convention. The area provides an important habitat for waterfowl and is a key habitat for numerous species, including the West Indian Manatee.

Pointe-à-Pierre Wildfowl Trust
The middle of an oil refinery may seem an odd place for a nature sanctuary, but this is one of the best bird viewing spots in Trinidad. This 62-acre (25-ha) site is part for wild birds and part for breeding cages for endangered species.

La Brea Pitch Lake
On the southwest tip of Trinidad is one of the world's few open pitch lakes from which this ingredient of asphalt has been mined and exported since 1859. Visitors to the site walk across the fairly solid surface of the lake.

OFFICIAL NAME
Republic of Trinidad and Tobago

LAND AREA
1,980 square miles (5,128 square km)

CAPITAL
Port-of-Spain

MAJOR PORTS
Pointe-à-Pierre, Point Fortin, Point Lisas, Port-of-Spain, Scarborough

MOUNTAIN RANGES
Mount Aripo, Mount Tamana, and Main Ridge

CLIMATE
Tropical; rainy season (June—December)

HIGHEST POINT
Aripo Mountain (3,084 feet/940 m)

COASTLINE
225 miles (362 km)

POPULATION
1,229,953 (2009 estimate)

LIFE EXPECTANCY
0—14 years: 19.6 percent
15—64 years: 72.6 percent
65 years and over: 7.8 percent (2009 estimate)

BIRTHRATE
14.36 births/1,000 Trinidadians/Tobagonians (2009 estimate)

ETHNIC GROUPS
Indian (South Asian) 40 percent, African 37.5 percent, mixed 20.5 percent, others 1.2 percent, and unspecified 0.8 percent

RELIGION
Roman Catholic 26 percent, Hindu 22.5 percent, Anglican 7.8 percent, Baptist 7.2 percent, Pentecostal 6.8 percent, Muslim 5.8 percent, Seventh-Day Adventist 4 percent, other Christian 5.8 percent, others 10.8 percent, unspecified 1.4 percent, and none 1.9 percent

LANGUAGES
English (official), Caribbean Hindustani (a dialect of Hindi), French, Spanish, and Chinese

NATIONAL HOLIDAY
Independence Day, February 24

TIME LINE

IN TRINIDAD AND TOBAGO	IN THE WORLD
Before 300 B.C. Hunter-gatherer Meso-Indians live on the island of Trinidad, leaving behind stone tools and shell middens.	
300 B.C. A second wave of settlers arrives on Tobago. They colonized most of the lesser Antilles and spoke dialects of the Arawak language.	
1000 Another group who can speak Carib dialects moves onto the islands.	**1206–1368** Genghis Khan unifies the Mongols and starts conquest of the world. At its height, the Mongol Empire under Kublai Khan stretches from China to Persia and parts of Europe and Russia.
1498 Christopher Columbus visits the islands, naming Trinidad after the three peaks at its southeast corner and Tobago after a local type of tobacco pipe.	
1532 Spain colonizes Trinidad, appointing a governor to rule it.	**1776** U.S. Declaration of Independence
1781 The French capture Tobago from the Spanish, transforming it into a sugar-producing colony.	**1789–99** The French Revolution
1797 A British naval expedition captures Trinidad from Spain.	
1802 Spain cedes Trinidad to Great Britain under the Treaty of Amiens.	
1814 France cedes Tobago to Great Britain.	
1834 Slavery abolished; indentured workers brought in from India to work on sugar plantations.	
1889 Trinidad and Tobago administratively combined as a single British colony.	**1914** World War I begins.
1958 Trinidad and Tobago joins the British-sponsored West Indies Federation.	**1939** World War II begins.
1959 Great Britain gives Trinidad and Tobago internal self-government with Williams as prime minister.	

IN TRINIDAD AND TOBAGO	IN THE WORLD
1962	
Trinidad and Tobago leaves the West Indies Federation; becomes independent with Williams as prime minister.	
1976	
Trinidad and Tobago becomes a republic with the former governor-general, Ellis Clarke, as president and Eric Williams as prime minister.	
1981	
Agriculture Minister George Chambers becomes prime minister following Williams's death.	
1986	
Tobago-based National Alliance for Reconstruction (NAR) headed by Arthur Robinson wins the general election.	
1987	
Noor Hassanali becomes president.	
1991	
Patrick Manning becomes prime minister after his PNM party wins general election.	
1995	
Indian-based United National Congress (UNC) and NAR form coalition with Basdeo Panday as prime minister.	**1997** Hong Kong is returned to China.
2000	
Basdeo Panday wins another term in general elections.	**2001** Terrorists crash planes into New York, Washington D.C., and Pennsylvania.
2002	
Prime Minister Patrick Manning's ruling People's National Movement wins elections.	
2003	**2003** War in Iraq begins.
President Maxwell Richards is sworn in after being elected by MPs in February.	
2007	
Plans are announced to close the centuries-old sugar industry.	
2010	
Kamla Persad-Bissessar is elected as the first female prime minister of Trinidad and Tobago.	

GLOSSARY

arboreal
Living in or among trees.

Callaloo (KAL-a-oo)
A creole dish made of salt beef, okra, and sweet potato leaves.

conurbation
An extensive urban area resulting from the expansion of several cities or towns so that they combine but usually retain their separate identities.

dhalpourri (dal-POUR-e)
A type of roti bread that is made using two layers of dough to form a thin sandwich.

Dih (DEE)
A spirit believed in by those who practice black magic.

Douens (DOO-ens)
According to those who practice black magic, these are the spirits of unbaptized children and they are malevolent.

Dougla
People of mixed Indian and African race.

Haile Selassie
The name of the former emperor of Ethiopia, whom the Rastafarians believe to be God.

imam
A religious Islamic man who leads prayers in the mosque.

jihad
A Muslim holy war.

mauby (MAO-by)
A nonalcoholic drink made from an extract of the mauby tree bark.

midden
A dunghill or trash heap.

muezzin
A man who calls Muslims to prayer from the mosque minaret.

mulattos
People of mixed race.

obeah
An African religious doctor who practices witchcraft and prescribes natural (herbal) medicine.

parang (par-ANG)
Traditional Christmas music evolved from Spanish carols.

parranderos (par-an-DARE-owes)
The musicians who perform parang.

pelau (PEL-ow)
A creole dish of chicken, vegetables, and peas, spiced by pepper, garlic, and onions.

puja (PU-ja)
A Hindu religious service that combines the worship of several deities at one time.

FOR FURTHER INFORMATION

BOOKS

Baksh, Solomon. *Trinidad And Tobago* (Macmillan Caribbean Dive Guides). Oxford, U.K.: MacMillan Caribbean, February 2006.

Besson, Gerard. *Folklore and Legends of Trinidad and Tobago.* Cascade, Trinidad: Paria Publishing Company Ltd, 2007.

Fredick, Malcolm (Author), Das, Prodeepta (Illustrator). *Kamal Goes to Trinidad* (Children Return to their Roots). London, U.K.: Frances Lincoln Children's Books, 2008.

Ganeshram, Ramin. *Sweet Hands: Island Cooking from Trinidad and Tobago.* New York: Hippocrene Books, 2010.

Hernandez, Romel. *Trinidad and Tobago* (The Caribbean Today). Broomall, PA: Mason Crest Publishers, 2009.

Kenefick, Martyn, Restall, Robin, Hayes, Floyd, *Field Guide to the Birds of Trinidad and Tobago.* New Haven, CT: Yale University Press, 2008.

Oliver, Merlin (Author), Copeland, Susan (Illustrator). *Of Marbles, Ice & Time: A Story of Trinidad.* Bloomington, IN: Trafford Publishing, 2006.

Smailes, Alex (Photographer), Taylor, Jeremy (Introduction). *Trinidad & Tobago: Carnival Land Water People.* Oxford, U.K.: MacMillan Caribbean, 2006.

FILMS

McComie, R. Barry. *NCBA/Samaroo's Kings & Queens of Trinidad & Tobago Carnival 2009.* Advance Dynamics Ltd, 2009.

Tacarigua: A Village in Trinidad and Tobago. 2010.

MUSIC

Steel Band of Trinidad/Tobago. *The Heart of Steel.* Rounder Records, 2009.

Al St. John's Trinidad & Tobago Steelband. *Caribbean Christmas Carnival.* Dynamic Recording, 2008.

Various Artists. *The Gathering: Trinidad & Tobago.* Lion of Zion Entertainment, 2009.

BIBLIOGRAPHY

BOOKS

Gordon, Lesley. *Insight Guide Trinidad & Tobago* (Insight Guides Trinidad and Tobago). London, U.K.: Insight Guides, 2005.

O'Donnell, Kathleen. *Adventure Guides to Trinidad & Tobago* (Adventure Guide to Trinidad & Tobago). Walpole, MA: Hunter Publishing, 2000.

Thomas, Polly. *The Rough Guide to Trinidad & Tobago* (Rough Guides). London, U.K.: Rough Guides, 2010.

Ver Berkmoes, Ryan, Porup, Jens, Grossberg. *Michael Caribbean Islands* (Multi Country Guide). Victoria, Australia: Lonely Planet Publications, 2008.

Warner, Keith. *The Trinidad Calypso.* London, U.K.: Heinemann, 1999.

Wood, Lawson. *Lonely Planet Diving & Snorkelling Trinidad & Tobago* (Lonely Planet Diving and Snorkelling Guides). Victoria, Australia: Lonely Planet Publications, 2000.

WEBSITES

Central Bank of Trinidad and Tobago, www.central-bank.org.tt/

CIA World Factbook Trinidad and Tobago, www.cia.gov/library/publications/the-world-factbook/geos/td.html

Countries of the World Trinidad and Tobago, www.theodora.com/wfbcurrent/trinidad_and_tobago/trinidad_and_tobago_economy.html

Environmental Management Authority Trinidad and Tobago, www.ema.co.tt/cms/

Infoplease Trinidad and Tobago, www.infoplease.com/ipa/A0108046.html

Lonely Planet Trinidad and Tobago Travel and Information Guide, www.lonelyplanet.com/trinidad-and-tobago

Nature Worldwide Trinidad and Tobago, www.nature-worldwide.info/trinidad_&_tobago.htm

Parks.it Trinidad and Tobago www.parks.it/world/TT/Eindex.html

Planetware Trinidad and Tobago Tourist Attractions, www.planetware.com/tourist-attractions-/trinidad-and-tobago-tri-tri-tt.htm

The Official Trinidad and Tobago Travel and Tourism Site, www.gotrinidadandtobago.com/

Tourist Attractions Trinidad and Tobago, www.whenwegetthere.com/tourist_destination_attraction/caribbean/trinidad_and_tobago/10_313/trinidad_and_tobago.jsp

Tourist Destinations in Trinidad and Tobago, http://travel.mapsofworld.com/trinidad-and-tobago/

Trinidad and Tobago Government Portal, www.ttconnect.gov.tt/gortt/portal/ttconnect

Trinidad and Tobago's Newsday, www.newsday.co.tt/news/0,72999.html

U.S. Department of State Trinidad and Tobago, www.state.gov/r/pa/ei/bgn/35638.htm

INDEX

INDEX